The Best of

E.M. BOUNDS

The Best of

E.M.
BOUNDS

120 DAILY DEVOTIONS
to NURTURE YOUR SPIRIT *and*
REFRESH YOUR SOUL

Edited and Compiled by Stephen W. Sorenson

Inspiration and Motivation for the Seasons of Life

COOK COMMUNICATIONS MINISTRIES
Colorado Springs, Colorado • Paris, Ontario
KINGSWAY COMMUNICATIONS LTD
Eastbourne, England

Honor® is an imprint of
Cook Communications Ministries, Colorado Springs, CO 80918
Cook Communications, Paris, Ontario
Kingsway Communications, Eastbourne, England

THE BEST OF E. M. BOUNDS
© 2006 by Cook Communications Ministries

Cover Design: Jackson Design CO, LLC/Greg Jackson

First Printing, 2006
Printed in the United States of America

        1 2 3 4 5 6 7 8 9 10 Printing/Year 10 09 08 07 06

Editor's note: The selections in this book have been "gently modern-
ized" for today's reader. Words, phrases, and sentence structure have
been updated for readability and clarity; new chapter headings and
Scripture verses have been combined with excerpts from E. M. Bounds'
text. Every effort has been made to preserve the integrity and intent of
Bounds' original writings. Reflection questions at the end of each reading have been included to aid in personal exploration and group
discussion.

ISBN-13: 978-1-56292-447-8
ISBN-10: 1-56292-447-8

LCCN: 2006929564

A Man of Quiet but Profound Influence

———◦◦◦◦———

During his lifetime, Edward McKendree Bounds (1835–1913) never attracted a large following, gained much notoriety, or achieved anything resembling fame. After five decades of faithful ministry, he was still virtually unknown to anyone beyond the communities where he served as pastor or itinerant evangelist. What's more, of the eight books he wrote on prayer, only two were published during his lifetime. Like countless other servants of the Lord through the ages, Bounds diligently lived out his faith without the expectation of earthly accolades or honors.

Given his humble life of service, it is perhaps ironic that today—a hundred years after his death—Bounds is widely recognized as a foremost thinker and writer on the subject of prayer. Numerous scholars, professors, and pastors revere Bounds as someone who plumbed the depths of prayer like few others before or after him.

As biographer David Smithers notes, "Though hidden and unrecognized while alive, E. M. Bounds is now considered by most evangelicals as the most prolific and fervent author on the subject of prayer."

Born in Shelby County, Missouri, Bounds was blessed to be raised by godly parents. His father was a successful businessman and a devoted Christian layman who was instrumental in establishing the First Methodist Church in Shelbyville. During his youth, E. M. attended local schools, and he persistently studied the Scriptures as well as the writings of John Wesley.

Hardship fell upon E. M. and his family in 1849 when his father contracted tuberculosis and died at the age of forty-four. E. M. was only fourteen years old. He later recounted how his father's death stirred in him a yearning to know God in a deeper, more personal way.

Still, professional ministry was a few years off. Not long after his father's death, E. M. and his older brother Charles ventured from Missouri to Mesquite Canyon, California, as part of the gold rush. Their dreams of quick and abundant riches were gradually dashed by the reality of harsh living conditions and long hours of back-breaking work with little remuneration. Worse, the Bounds brothers were appalled by the moral degradation of their fellow miners, who frequented brothels, saloons, and gambling halls. After four unsuccessful years, E. M. and Charles returned home.

Back in Missouri, Bounds studied law and, at age twenty-one, became the state's youngest practicing attorney. He continued as a lawyer for four years until he felt called to full-time ministry. Ordained in 1859, he was named pastor of a small Methodist congregation in Monticello, Missouri.

When the Civil War began two years later, Bounds joined the Confederate States Army as a chaplain. Early on he was imprisoned with hundreds of other noncombatants and endured terrible prison conditions for a month and a half. When released, he traveled more than a hundred miles on foot to join up with the Third Missouri Infantry.

Despite his humble demeanor, Bounds proved to be a man of great courage. As a chaplain he could have remained safely away from the frontlines, but he chose to stay with the soldiers in the heat of battle. He found himself in the midst of many fierce campaigns and witnessed firsthand the horrors of war. Indeed, against the urging of fellow chaplains, Bounds remained in Vicksburg during the siege and ministered to war-ravaged citizens and soldiers.

Between battles Bounds would preach at local churches, where numerous townspeople and soldiers became Christians, and many more received comfort because of his heartfelt ministry. According to historian Charles Jennings, Bounds later survived the battle of Atlanta and the massacre at Franklin, Tennessee, where he received a severe head injury from a Union saber. He was taken prisoner a second time after the Franklin campaign and held until he pledged his allegiance to the Union.

Upon his release he felt compelled to minister in war-torn Franklin and help rebuild it spiritually. Bounds was recognized as a leader in the spiritual revival of the city. After several years of service there, he went on to pastor other Tennessee churches, along with some in Alabama and St. Louis, Missouri. During these years, Bounds also served as associate editor of the *Christian Advocate*, the publication of the Methodist Episcopal Church, South.

At the age of forty-one he married Emma Barnett, and the couple had three children. Nine years later, at the age of thirty, Emma died unexpectedly, leaving Bounds deep in mourning. Nearly two years later Bounds remarried, this time to a cousin of his first wife named Harriet Barnett. Fifty-two years old at the time of his second marriage, E. M. went on to have four children with Harriet. In the years ahead E. M. would suffer more heartache as he lost two of his children—Edwards Jr. and Charles—to illness.

Through all the events of Bounds' life, both tragic and tranquil, prayer served as his foundation. In his sermons and writings Bounds would often refer to the "work of prayer," and he approached his own prayer life with utmost discipline. Rising each morning at 4:00 a.m., he spent a minimum of three to four hours every day in fervent prayer. Friends and ministry colleagues recalled their amazement at his ability to stay on his knees in prayer, often weeping as he did, for hours at a time. For Bounds, prayer was not preparation for ministry endeavors; it was the highest form of ministry. Prayer for him was not a preamble to the day's activities; it was the principal activity of the day.

As he grew older, Bounds spoke out more forcefully against the slackening moral standards among Christians, especially Christian leaders. His call for uncompromised holiness made many uncomfortable and caused rifts between himself and other leaders in his denomination. He once wrote, "What the church needs today is not better machinery and operations, not new programs and plans, not more efficient methods and organizations. What the church needs are people whom the Holy Spirit can use—people fully surrendered to God, people devoted to holiness, people willing to sacrifice all for the cause of Christ. The Holy Spirit does not flow through methods, but through people. He does not dwell in machinery, but in people. He does not anoint plans, but godly people."

In his latter years Bounds devoted himself to writing, primarily on prayer. His works include *Power through Prayer* and *The Weapon of Prayer*, which are now considered classics. Because he so diligently practiced what he preached, his insights and passion reverberate today, inspiring believers to higher standards of discipleship and a more powerful prayer life.

Prayer's Double Blessing

"I exhort first of all that supplications, prayers, intercessions, and giving of thanks be made for all men ... that we may lead a quiet and peaceable life in all godliness and reverence."

1 TIMOTHY 2:1–2

Prayer reaches up to heaven and brings heaven down to earth. Prayer has in its hands a double blessing: It rewards him who prays and blesses him who is prayed for. It brings peace to warring passions and calms warring elements. Tranquility is the happy fruit of true praying. There is an inner calm that comes to him who prays and an outer calm as well. Prayer creates quiet and peaceable lives "in all godliness and reverence."

Right praying not only makes life beautiful in peace, but redolent in righteousness and weighty in influence as well. Honesty, gravity, integrity, and weight in character are the natural and essential fruits of prayer.

Reflection

How has prayer calmed you during stressful times? What blessings has God given you as a result of your prayers?

2

Pursue God Every Morning

"My voice You shall hear in the morning, O LORD; in the morning
I will direct it to You, and I will look up."

PSALM 5:3

The person who fritters away the early morning—its opportunity and freshness—in other pursuits than seeking God will make poor headway seeking Him the rest of the day. If God is not first in our thoughts and efforts in the morning, He will be in the last place the remainder of the day.

Behind this early rising and early praying is the ardent desire that presses us into this pursuit after God. Morning listlessness is the sign of a listless heart. The heart that is sluggish in seeking God in the morning has lost its relish for God.

Our laziness after God is our crying sin. The children of this world are far wiser than we are. They are at it early and late. We do not seek God with ardor and diligence. No man gets God who does not follow hard after Him, and no person follows hard after God who is not after Him during the first moments of the day.

Reflection

Why is it so easy to be lazy concerning our relationship with God? What specific things hinder you from pursuing God first thing in the morning?

Our Prayers Influence God

"Call to Me, and I will answer you, and show you great and mighty things, which you do not know."

JEREMIAH 33:3

Prayer puts God's work in His hands and keeps it there. It looks to Him constantly and depends on Him implicitly to further His own cause. Prayer is but faith resting in, acting with, and leaning on God. This is why God loves it so much, why He puts all power into its hands, and why He so highly esteems men of prayer.

Everywhere in His Word, God's actions and attitude are shaped by prayer. To quote all the scriptural passages that prove the immediate, direct, and personal relation of prayer to God would be to transfer whole pages of the Scripture to this study. Man has personal relations with God. Prayer is the divinely appointed means by which man comes into direct connection with God. By His own ordinance, God holds Himself bound to hear prayer. God bestows His great good on His children when they seek it along the avenue of prayer.

Reflection

In what ways do you think prayer "influences" God? Which things in your life do you need to put into "God's hands" today?

Maintain Loyalty to Christ

"If you were of the world, the world would love its own. Yet because you are not of the world, but I chose you out of the world, therefore the world hates you."

JOHN 15:19

Heaven is Christ's place, the place where He is and to which He would win men. The world is Satan's place. His power is here. To fix our hearts on the world is to be loyal to him. To fix our hearts on heaven is to be loyal to Christ.

Here we have the reasons for the world's cruel hatred of Jesus and why it has persecuted His followers so bitterly, even unto death. The Devil is in the flesh and rules it. Christ is in the Spirit. This world leads away from Christ. It is the invincible foe of Christ.

This great truth is illustrated and enforced by the fact that Christ's work is to get possession of the world and make its attractive power further His purposes. But He establishes a kingdom of heaven that is not of this world. A new power has come in, a new kingdom established, and a new world made. It will take the fires of the judgment and the new creative power to make a new heaven and a new earth before the stains and ruin of the Devil's debasing and death-dealing hands can be removed and this alien world is fitted for God's holy purposes.

The Christian, by the urgent demand made on him to swear allegiance to the world, is by his very relationship to Jesus Christ lifted out of the world's deadly embraces, and its polluting blights are broken.

Reflection

In what ways have you experienced the world's animosity because of your loyalty to Christ? What does it mean to "fix your heart" on heaven?

5

The Perils of Prayerlessness

"The LORD said: 'I have surely seen the oppression of My people who are in Egypt, and have heard their cry because of their taskmasters, for I know their sorrows. So I have come down to deliver them out of the hand of the Egyptians.'"

EXODUS 3:7–8

Nothing is more important to God than prayer in dealing with mankind. But it is likewise all-important for man to pray. Failure to pray is failure along the whole line of life. It is failure of duty, service, and spiritual progress. God must help man by prayer. The person who does not pray, therefore, robs himself of God's help and places God where He cannot help man. Man must pray to God if love for God is to exist. Faith, hope, patience, and all the strong, vital forces of piety are withered and dead in a prayerless life. The blessings to the individual believer have their being, bloom, and fruitfulness in prayer.

All this and much more can be said concerning the necessity of prayer to the being and pursuit of piety in the individual. But prayer has a larger sphere, a more obligated duty, a loftier inspiration. God's will and glory are bound up in praying. The days of God's splendor and renown have always been the great days of prayer. God's great movements in this world have been conditioned on, continued by, and fashioned by prayer. God has put Himself in these great movements just as men have prayed. Present, prevailing, conspicuous, and persistent prayer has always brought God to be present. The real and obvious test of a genuine work of God is the prevalence of the spirit of prayer. God's movement to bring Israel from Egyptian bondage had its inception in prayer. Thus early did God and the human race establish the fact of prayer as one of the granite forces on which His world movements were to be based.

Reflection

Do you really believe that your prayers are important to God? Why or why not? What happens in the life of a believer who doesn't pray?

A Strong Church Is a Praying Church

"And they prayed and said, 'You, O Lord, who know the hearts of all, show which of these two You have chosen to take part in this ministry.'"

ACTS 1:24–25

When the church is in the condition of prayer, God's cause always flourishes and His kingdom on earth always triumphs. When the church fails to pray, God's cause decays and evil of every kind prevails. In other words, God works through the prayers of His people, and when they fail Him at this point, decline and deadness ensue.

It is according to the divine plans that spiritual prosperity comes through the prayer channel. Praying saints are God's agents for carrying on His saving and providential work on earth. If His agents fail Him, neglecting to pray, then His work fails. Praying agents of the Most High are always forerunners of spiritual prosperity.

Through the ages, Christians who have held the church for God have had in fullness and richness the ministry of prayer. The leaders of the church whom the Scriptures reveal have had preeminence in prayer. Eminent they may have been in culture, in intellect, and in all the natural or human forces; or they may have been lowly in physical attainments and native gifts. Yet in each case, prayer was the all-potent force in the leadership of the church. This was so because God was with and in what they did, because prayer always carries us back to God. It recognizes God and brings Him into the world to work, save, and bless. The most efficient agents in disseminating the knowledge of God, in executing His work on the earth, and in standing as breakwater against the billows of evil have been praying church leaders. God depends on them, employs them, and blesses them.

Reflection

Why do you think God's most efficient agents on earth are praying people? What are some reasons why people in the church fail to pray?

A Secret of Spiritual Power

*"Grace and peace be multiplied to you in the knowledge of God
and of Jesus our Lord, as His divine power has given to us
all things that pertain to life and godliness."*

2 PETER 1:2–3

No amount of money, genius, or culture can move things for God. Holiness energizing the soul, the whole man aflame with love and with desire for more faith, zeal, and consecration—this is the secret of power. These we need and must have, and men must be the incarnation of this God-inflamed devotedness.

God's advance has been stayed, His cause crippled, and His name dishonored from a lack of fervor and devotion among His people. Intellect, education, wealth, position, celebrity, status, and renown cannot move the chariot of our God. Wholehearted devotion to Him can and will.

Reflection

How do these "secrets of power" compare to those espoused by our society? To what extent are you experiencing God's power in your life?

The Imperative of Prayer

"Pray without ceasing."
1 THESSALONIANS 5:17

No insistence in the Scriptures is more pressing than prayer. No exhortation is more often reiterated, none is more hearty, none is more solemn and stirring than to pray. No principle is more strongly and broadly declared than that which urges us to pray. There is no duty to which we are more strongly obliged than the obligation to pray. There is no command more imperative and insistent than that of praying.

Are you praying in everything without ceasing, in the closet, hidden from the eyes of men, and praying always and everywhere? That is the personal, pertinent, and all-important question for every person.

Reflection

When are you most motivated to pray? Why? What in God's character causes our prayers to be so important to Him?

The Link between Prayer and the Spirit

"When they had prayed, the place where they were assembled together was shaken; and they were all filled with the Holy Spirit."

ACTS 4:31

Praying people are the only people who have influence with God, the only kind of people to whom God commits Himself and His mission. Praying people are the only people in which the Holy Spirit dwells, for the Holy Spirit and prayer go hand in hand. The Holy Spirit never descends upon prayerless people. He never fills them; He never empowers them. There is nothing whatever in common between the Spirit of God and people who do not pray. The Spirit dwells only in a prayer atmosphere.

Reflection

Why is prayer essential to the filling and empowerment of the Holy Spirit? How would you describe the link between prayer and the Spirit?

Give Thanks to God

"We give thanks to You, O God, we give thanks!"

PSALM 75:1

Gratitude and thanksgiving always look back at the past, though they may also take in the present. But prayer always looks to the future. Thanksgiving deals with things already received. Prayer deals with things desired, asked for, and expected. Prayer turns to gratitude and praise when God has granted the things asked for.

Gratitude and thanksgiving forever stand opposed to all murmurings at God's dealings with us and all complaining about our lot. Gratitude and murmuring never abide in the same heart at the same time. An unappreciative spirit has no standing beside gratitude and praise. And true prayer corrects complaining and promotes gratitude. Dissatisfaction with one's lot, and a disposition to be discontented with things that come to us in God's providence, are foes of gratitude and enemies of thanksgiving.

Grumblers are ungrateful people. Appreciative men and women have neither the time nor disposition to stop and complain. The bane of the wilderness journey of the Israelites on their way to Canaan was their propensity to complain against God and Moses. For this, God was several times greatly grieved, and it took the strong praying of Moses to avert God's anger because of these murmurings. The absence of gratitude left no room or disposition for praise and thanksgiving, just as it is always so. But when these same Israelites were brought through the Red Sea with dry feet while their enemies were destroyed, Miriam, the sister of Moses, led a song of praise. Prayer and gratitude are intertwined and, when practiced together regularly, lift our eyes toward heaven.

Reflection

How often do you catch yourself complaining and grumbling? How might you develop a deeper attitude of thankfulness and express that in your prayers?

Prayer for Ministry Is Essential

"Brethren, pray for us."
1 THESSALONIANS 5:25

If Paul was so dependent on the prayers of God's saints to give his ministry success, how much more important is it that the prayers of God's saints be centered on the ministry of today!

Paul did not feel that this urgent plea for prayer would lower his dignity, lessen his influence, or depreciate his piety. What if it did? Let dignity go, let influence be destroyed, and let his reputation be marred—he needed their prayers. Called, commissioned, chief of the apostles as Paul was, all of his equipment was imperfect without the prayers of his people. He regularly wrote letters, urging them to pray for him.

Do you pray for your pastor? Do you pray for leaders in your church and other ministries? Do you pray for missionaries and Christian workers everywhere? If not, begin doing so today. For their effectiveness in ministry will be bolstered because of such prayer support.

Reflection

Why do you think Paul asked so many early Christians to pray for him? Which leaders might you pray for today?

The Power of Persevering Prayer

"When Daniel knew that the writing was signed, he went home. And in his upper room, with his windows open toward Jerusalem, he knelt down on his knees three times that day, and prayed and gave thanks before his God, as was his custom since early days."

DANIEL 6:10

Persevering prayer always wins, for God yields to persistence and diligence when based on sincere trust in Him. In Babylon, Daniel refused to obey the king's decree not to ask any petition of any god or man for thirty days. Daniel shut his eyes to the decree that would shut him off from his praying room. He would not be deterred from calling on God.

There was nothing impersonal about Daniel's praying. It always had an objective and was an appeal to a great God who could do all things. There was no coddling of self, nor looking after subjective or reflex influences. In the face of the dreadful decree that would hasten him from a place of power and into the lion's den, he "knelt down on his knees three times that day, and prayed and gave thanks before his God, as was his custom since early days." The gracious result was that prayer laid its hands on an Almighty arm, which interposed in that den of vicious, cruel lions and closed their mouths and preserved His servant Daniel, who had been true to Him and who had called on Him for protection. Daniel's praying was an essential factor in defeating the king's decree and in embarrassing the wicked, envious rulers who had set the trap for Daniel in order to destroy him and remove him from power in the kingdom.

Reflection

What does "persevering in prayer" involve? Think about your prayer life and the extent to which you do or don't persevere in prayer. What role should persevering prayer play in facing difficult challenges?

Expect Intense Spiritual Warfare

"Put on the whole armor of God, that you may be able to stand against the wiles of the devil."

EPHESIANS 6:11

It cannot be stated too frequently that the life of a Christian involves warfare, an intense conflict, a lifelong contest. It is a battle, moreover, waged against invisible foes who are always seeking to entrap, deceive, and ruin the souls of men. The life to which Holy Scripture calls men is no picnic or holiday trip. It is no pastime, no pleasure jaunt. It entails effort, wrestling, and struggling. It demands the putting forth of the full energy of the Spirit in order to frustrate the foe and to come off, at the last, more than a conqueror. It is no primrose path, no rose-scented dalliance. From start to finish, it is war. From the hour in which he first draws sword, to that in which he doffs his harness, the Christian warrior is compelled to "endure hardship as a good soldier" (2 Tim. 2:3).

What a misconception many people have of the Christian life! How little the average church member appears to understand the character of the conflict and its demands. How ignorant he seems to be of the enemies he must encounter if he seeks to serve God faithfully and thus succeed in getting to heaven and receive the crown of life. He seems scarcely to realize that the world, the flesh, and the Devil will oppose his onward march and will defeat him utterly, unless he gives himself to constant vigilance and unceasing prayer.

Reflection

Why do so many Christians misunderstand the nature of spiritual warfare and its effect on their lives? What are you doing to remain strong against the enemies of God?

Too Busy to Pray?

"Epaphras, who is one of you, a bondservant of Christ, greets you, always laboring fervently for you in prayers."

COLOSSIANS 4:12

Sacred work—church activities—may so engage and absorb us as to hinder praying. When this is the case, evil results always follow. It is better to let the work go by default than to let the praying go by neglect. Whatever affects the intensity of our praying affects the value of our work. "Too busy to pray" is not only the keynote to backsliding, but it also undermines the work done. Nothing is well done without prayer for the simple reason that it leaves God out of the picture.

How easily are we led by Satan's insidious wiles to cut short our praying in the interests of the work. How easy it is to neglect prayer or abbreviate our praying simply by the plea that we have church work on our hands. Satan has effectively disarmed us when he can keep us too busy doing things to stop and pray.

It is not only the sinful things that hurt prayer or questionable things that are to be guarded against. It is things that are right in their places but are allowed to sidetrack prayer, often with the self-comforting plea that "we are too busy to pray."

Reflection

Which activities tend to sidetrack you from praying? Do you often feel too busy to pray? What can you do to regulate your schedule and adjust your priorities?

Seek to Know and Glorify God

"And now, O Father, glorify Me together with Yourself, with the glory which I had with You before the world was."

JOHN 17:5

Let us stop and ask: Do we know God tentatively and remotely, or do we know Him deeply and personally? Do we know Jesus Christ as a person and as a personal Savior? Do we know Him by a heart acquaintance and know Him well? A deep, abiding love relationship is what God seeks with us.

Let us further ask: Is Jesus glorified in us? Do our lives prove His divinity? And does Jesus shine brighter because of us? Are we opaque or transparent bodies, and do we darken or reflect His pure light? Do we seek glory where Christ sought it? Do we esteem the presence and possession of God, our most excellent glory and our supreme good?

In all we do—in thought and deed—let us seek to know God more deeply and to glorify Him more fully.

Reflection

Is your life bringing glory to God? If not, why not? What specifically is involved in "seeking God's glory"?

The Bible: A Book of Prayer

"I entreated Your favor with my whole heart; be merciful to me according to Your word."

PSALM 119:58

As God's house is called "the house of prayer" because prayer is the most important of its holy offices, so by the same token the Bible may be called the book of prayer. Prayer is the great theme and content of its message to mankind.

God's Word is the basis, as it is the directory, of the prayer of faith. "Let the word of Christ dwell in you richly in all wisdom," says Paul (Col. 3:16). As this word of Christ dwelling in us richly is transmuted and assimilated, it issues forth in praying. Faith is constructed of the Word and the Spirit, and faith is the body and substance of prayer.

In many of its aspects, prayer is dependent on God's Word. Jesus said, "If you abide in Me, and My words abide in you, you will ask what you desire, and it shall be done for you" (John 15:7). The Word of God is the fulcrum on which the lever of prayer is placed and by which things are mightily moved. God has committed Himself, His purpose, and His promise to prayer. His Word becomes the basis—the inspiration—of our praying, and there are circumstances under which we may obtain an addition or an enlargement of His promises. It is said of the old saints that they "through faith ... obtained promises" (Heb. 11:33).

Reflection

Think of some ways in which prayer is dependent on God's Word. Which biblical promises might God want you to appropriate when you pray?

God's Amazing Promises

"Whatever things you ask in prayer, believing, you will receive."
MATTHEW 21:22

This all-comprehensive condition not only presses us to pray for all things, everything great and small, but it brings us closer to God. For who but God can assure us certainly of receiving the very thing for which we may ask in all the thesaurus of earthly and heavenly good?

Jesus Christ, the Son of God, makes demands on us to pray, and He puts Himself and all He has so fully in the answer. He puts Himself at our service and answers our demands when we pray.

Just as He puts Himself and the Father at our command in prayer, to come directly into our lives and work for our good, so also does He engage to answer the requests of two or more believers who are agreed on their desires. "If two of you agree on earth concerning anything that they ask, it will be done for them by My Father in heaven" (Matt. 18:19). No one but God could put Himself in a covenant so binding as that, because only God could fulfill such a promise and could reach to its exacting and all-controlling demands. Only God can answer for the promises.

Reflection

Which of God's promises mean the most to you? In what ways has God kept His promises in your life recently?

The Problem with Prosperity

"Some trust in chariots, and some in horses; but we will remember the name of the LORD our God."

PSALM 20:7

This is the day of great wealth in the church and of wonderful material resources. But unfortunately, affluence and prosperity are enemies and a severe hindrance to strong spiritual forces. It is an invariable law that the presence of attractive and potent material forces creates a trust in them—and by the same inevitable law creates distrust in the spiritual forces of the gospel.

Material forces and spiritual forces are two masters that cannot be served at one and the same time. For just in proportion as the mind is fixed on one will it be drawn away from the other. The days of great financial prosperity in the church have not been days of great spiritual prosperity.

Reflection

How have material resources, including money, influenced you? What can you do to ensure that you are putting your trust in God rather than in material things?

Be Powerful and Prayerful

"Endure hardship as a good soldier of Jesus Christ."
2 TIMOTHY 2:3

Brave people, true people, praying people—afraid of nothing but God—are the kind needed now. There will be no smiting the forces of evil that now hold the world in bondage, no lifting of the degraded hordes of paganism to light and eternal life by any but praying people. All others are merely playing at religion, make-believe soldiers with no armor and no ammunition. None but soldiers and bondservants of Jesus Christ can possibly do this tremendous work. "Endure hardship as a good soldier of Jesus Christ" cries the great apostle.

This is no time to think about self, to pursue self-promotion, to seek comfort and ease; nor is it the time to shrink from hardship, grief, and loss. This is the time for toil, suffering, and self-denial. We must lose all for Christ in order to gain all for Christ.

Reflection

Are you a courageous warrior involved in the spiritual battle or a "make-believe" soldier? Why do you think suffering and hardship often accompany God's most mighty soldiers?

Be Rooted in God's Word

*"The entirety of Your word is truth, ...
My heart stands in awe of Your word."*
PSALM 119:160–161

One urgent need of our day is for people whose faith, prayers, and study of the Word of God have been vitalized and who will give it forth as the incorruptible seed that lives and abides forever. Nothing more is needed to clear up the haze by which a critical unfaith has eclipsed the Word of God than the fidelity of the pulpit in its unwavering allegiance to the Bible and the fearless proclamation of its truth. Without this, the standard-bearer fails, and wavering and confusion all along the ranks follow. The pulpit has wrought its mightiest work during the days of its unswerving loyalty to the Word of God.

Reflection

Why is it so important for every believer to proclaim biblical truth in love and sincerity to people who don't yet know God? When people stop viewing the Bible as the foundation of absolute truth, what consequences occur?

Focus on Today's Needs

"Give us this day our daily bread."

MATTHEW 6:11

When we pray "Give us this day our daily bread," we are, in a measure, shutting tomorrow out of our prayer. We do not live in the future but in present. We do not seek tomorrow's grace or tomorrow's bread. People thrive best, and get most out of life, who live fully *today*. They pray best who pray for today's needs, not for tomorrow's.

True prayers are born of present trials and present needs. Bread for today is bread enough. Bread given for today is the strongest sort of pledge that there will be bread tomorrow. Victory today is the assurance of victory tomorrow. Our prayers need to be focused on the present. We must trust God today and leave tomorrow entirely with Him. The present is ours; the future belongs to God. Prayer is the task and duty of each recurring day—daily prayer for daily needs.

As every day demands its bread, every day demands its prayer. No amount of praying, done today, will suffice for tomorrow's praying. On the other hand, no praying for tomorrow is of any great value to us today. Today's manna is what we need; tomorrow God will see that our needs are supplied. This is the faith that God seeks to inspire. So leave tomorrow, with its cares and needs and troubles, in His hands.

Reflection

How well are you doing at praying today for today's needs? What is the balance between focusing on today's needs and prudently planning for tomorrow's needs?

Aspire to Holiness

"I desire therefore that the men pray everywhere, lifting up holy hands."
1 TIMOTHY 2:8

There are certain conditions laid down for authentic praying. Men are to pray "lifting up holy hands"—hands here being symbolic for the entirety of one's life. Hands unsoiled by stains of evildoing are the emblem of a life unsoiled by sin. Thus are men to come into God's presence, thus are they to approach the throne of the Highest where they can "obtain mercy and find grace to help in time of need" (Heb. 4:16). Here, then, is one reason why men do not pray. They are too worldly in heart and too secular in life to enter the prayer closet. Even if they do enter, they cannot offer the "effective, fervent prayer of a righteous man," which "avails much" (James 5:16).

Hands, too, are symbols of activity, usefulness, and conduct. Hands outstretched to God in prayer must be "holy hands," unstained hands. The word *holy* here means undefiled, unspotted, untainted, and religiously observing every obligation. Prayer is sensitive and always affected by the character and conduct of the person who prays. Water cannot rise above its own level, and a spotless prayer cannot flow from a spotted heart. Straight praying is never born of crooked conduct. The craven heart cannot do brave praying. Soiled men cannot make clean, pure supplication.

Words matter little to the quality of prayer. What matters are character and conduct. When they are at low ebb, praying can but barely live, much less thrive. Praying receives its tone and vigor from the life of the man or woman exercising it.

Reflection

Are any sinful areas of your life hindering your prayer life? If so, what will you do about them? What is *holiness*, and how does it evidence itself in daily life?

Represent God in the Workplace

"Seek the LORD and His strength; seek His face evermore!"
PSALM 105:4

There is great need in this day for Christian businesspeople to inform their mundane affairs with the spirit of prayer and consecration to God. There is a great army of successful merchants and managers of almost every kind who are members of Christ's church, and it is crucial that these men and women attend to this matter. They must seek the realization and restraint of His presence and guidance in the workplace.

We need the atmosphere of godly devotion to pervade our factories, banks, and shops. We need the spirit of Sunday carried over to Monday—and continued throughout the week. We need businesspeople to go about their concerns with the same reverence and responsibility with which they engage in the most sacred religious activities.

Reflection

What happens when Christians make "religious" versus "secular" distinctions and basically try to keep God out of their typical workdays? In what ways can you represent God in the workplace?

Pray Diligently for Others

"Brethren, my heart's desire and prayer to God for Israel is that they may be saved."

ROMANS 10:1

Intercession for others is the hallmark of all true prayer. When prayer is confined to self and one's personal needs, it dies by reason of its littleness, narrowness, and selfishness. Prayer must be broad and unselfish, or it will perish. Prayer is the soul of a man stirred to plead with God for men. In addition to being interested in the eternal interests of one's own soul, it must be concerned about the spiritual and eternal welfare of others. One's ability to pray for self finds its climax in the compassion its concern expresses for other people.

The royal way to enlarge personal grace is to pray for others. Intercessory prayer is a means of grace to those who exercise it. We enter the richest fields of spiritual growth and gather its priceless riches in the avenues of intercessory prayer. To pray for people is of divine significance and represents the highest form of Christian service.

Reflection

Which people at work, in your neighborhood, and in your family might you begin to pray for regularly? Ask God to bring people to mind for whom you can intercede in prayer.

God Will Meet Our Needs

*"My God shall supply all your need according to
His riches in glory by Christ Jesus."*

PHILIPPIANS 4:19

God has much to do with believing people who have a living, transforming faith in Jesus Christ. These are God's children. A father loves his children, supplies their needs, hears their cries, and answers their requests. A child believes his father, loves him, trusts in him, and asks him for what he needs, without doubting that his father will hear his requests. God has everything to do with answering the prayers of His children. He is never happier than when answering their prayers.

Prayer covers the whole range of man's need. Hence, "in everything by prayer and supplication" are "requests [to] be made known to God (Phil. 4:6). Prayer includes the entire range of God's ability. "Is anything too hard for the LORD?" (Gen. 18:14). Prayer belongs to no favored segment of man's need, but reaches to and embraces the entire circle of his wants simply because God is the God of the whole man. God has pledged Himself to supply the needs of the whole man— physical, intellectual, and spiritual.

Reflection

How often do you bring your obvious and secret needs to God? What beliefs concerning God may be limiting your willingness to approach Him with your needs?

Pray Earnestly and Passionately

"They cried out to the LORD and said, 'We pray, O LORD, please do not let us perish for this man's life.'"

JONAH 1:14

Languid praying—without heart or strength, with neither fire nor tenacity—defeats its own avowed purpose. The prophet of ancient times lamented that in a day that needed strenuous praying, there was no one who "stirs himself up to take hold" of God (Isa. 64:7). Christ charged us not to "lose heart" in our praying (Luke 18:1). Laxity and indifference are great hindrances to prayer, both to the practice of praying and the process of receiving. It requires a brave, strong, fearless, and insistent spirit to engage in successful prayer.

Diffuseness, too, interferes with effectiveness. Too many petitions break tension and unity, and breed neglect. Prayers should be specific and urgent. Too many words, like too much width, breed shallows and sandbars. A single objective, which absorbs the whole being and animates the entire man, is the properly constraining force in prayer.

A breed of Christian is greatly needed who will seek tirelessly after God—who will give Him no rest, day and night, until He hearkens to their cry. The times demand praying people who are thirsty for God's glory, who are broad and unselfish in their desires, quenchless for God, who seek Him late and early, and who will give themselves no rest until the whole earth is filled with His glory.

Men and women are needed whose prayers will give to the world the utmost power of God, who will make His promises blossom with rich and full results. God is waiting to hear us.

Reflection

What makes prayer earnest and passionate instead of languid and lethargic? Have you "lost heart" in any area of life and stopped praying about it?

Cultivate Humility

"For by grace you have been saved through faith, and that not of yourselves; it is the gift of God, not of works, lest anyone should boast."

EPHESIANS 2:8–9

Happy are those who have no righteousness of their own to plead and no goodness of their own of which to boast. Humility flourishes in the soil of a true and deep sense of our sinfulness and our dependence on God. Nowhere does humility grow so rapidly and shine so brilliantly as when it acknowledges all weakness, confesses all sin, and trusts all grace.

God dwells in the lowly places. He makes such lowly places really the high places to the humble soul. The pride of doing sends its poison all through our praying. The same pride of being infects all our prayers, no matter how well worded they may be. This lack of humility, this self-applauding, this self-exaltation kept the most religious man of Christ's day from being accepted by God (see Luke 18:10–14). And the same thing will keep us in this day from being accepted by Him.

Reflection

Why is pride so easily developed and so difficult to get rid of? How is humility demonstrated in everyday life?

Who Needs God?

"They say to God, 'Depart from us, for we do not desire the knowledge of Your ways. Who is the Almighty, that we should serve Him? And what profit do we have if we pray to Him'?"

JOB 21:14–15

Prayer is the language of a person burdened with a sense of need. It is the voice of the beggar who is conscious of his poverty and asking another person for things he needs. It is not only the language of lack, but of felt lack, of lack consciously realized. "Blessed are the poor in spirit" means not only that the fact of poverty of spirit brings the blessing, but also that poverty of spirit is realized, known, and acknowledged (Matt. 5:3).

Prayer is the language of those who need something—something that they themselves cannot supply, but which God has promised them and for which they ask. In the end poor praying and prayerlessness amount to the same thing. Poor praying proceeds from a lack of the sense of need; prayerlessness has its origin in the same soil. Not to pray is not only to declare there is nothing needed, but to betray an ignorance of that need. This is what aggravates the sin of prayerlessness. It represents an attempt at instituting an independence of God, a self-sufficient ruling of God out of the life. It is a declaration made to God that we do not need Him and hence do not pray to Him.

Reflection

What does your prayer life reveal about your need for God and what He desires to provide? In what ways has the church today promoted aspects of personal independence that are not biblical?

Enriching Our Spiritual Relationship

——————

"I chose you and appointed you that you should go and bear fruit, and that your fruit should remain, that whatever you ask the Father in My name He may give you."

JOHN 15:16

Prayer is based not simply on a promise, but on a relationship. The returning penitent sinner prays on a promise. The child of God prays on the relationship of a child. What the Father has belongs to the child for present and prospective uses. The child asks; the Father gives. The relationship is one of asking and answering, of giving and receiving. The child is dependent on the Father, must look to the Father, must ask of the Father, and must receive of the Father.

We know how with earthly parents asking and giving belong to this relation, and how in the very act of asking and giving the relationship between parent and child is cemented, sweetened, and enriched. The parent finds a wealth of pleasure and satisfaction in giving to an obedient child, and the child finds wealth in the parent's loving and continuous giving. So it is in the spiritual realm, as the relationship between child and Father is deepened and developed through continued giving and receiving.

Reflection

How do you think God feels when His children come to Him with their sincere desires? Why? What are some ways, in addition to prayer, that you can deepen your relationship with the Father?

Faith Requires Patient Trust

*"Then Jesus said to them plainly, 'Lazarus is dead. And I am glad for your sakes that I was not there, that you may believe.' ...
And he who had died came out."*

JOHN 11:14–15, 44

Faith does not grow disheartened because prayer is not immediately honored. It takes God at His word and lets Him take what time He chooses in fulfilling His purposes and in carrying out His work. There is bound to be much delay and long days of waiting for true faith, but faith accepts the conditions, knows there will be delays in answering prayer, and regards such delays as times of testing in which faith is deepened.

The case of Lazarus was an instance of where there was delay, where the faith of two good women was sorely tried. Lazarus was critically ill, and his sisters sent for Jesus. But without any known reason, our Lord delayed His going to help His sick friend. Furthermore, our Lord's tardiness appeared to bring about hopeless disaster. While Jesus tarried, Lazarus died. But Jesus' delay was exercised in the interests of a greater good.

Fear not, tempted and tried believer, Jesus will come if patience is exercised and faith held fast. His delay will serve to make His coming the more richly blessed. Pray on. Wait on. If Christ delays, wait for Him. In His own good time, He will come. Faith gathers strength by waiting and praying. Patience has its perfect work in the school of delay. In some instances, delay is of the very essence of the prayer. God has to do many things before giving the final answer, things that are essential to the lasting good of the person who is requesting favor at His hands.

Reflection

What choices do we have when answers to our prayers seem to be delayed? How does our belief in the character of God influence our day-to-day choices?

Wanted: Devout and Devoted Leaders

"A bishop then must be blameless."
1 TIMOTHY 3:2

The present-day church has vast machinery. Its activities are great, and its material prosperity is unparalleled. The name of religion is widely spread and well known. Much money comes into the Lord's treasury and is paid out. But here is the question: Does the work of holiness keep pace with all this? Is the burden of the prayers of church people to be made holy? Are our pastors and leaders really holy people? Or to go back a little further, are they hungering and thirsting after righteousness, desiring the sincere milk of the Word that they may grow thereby (see 1 Peter 2:2)? Are they really seeking to be consecrated and devout?

Of course men of intelligence are greatly needed in the pulpit, but primary to it is the fact that we need holy men to stand before dying men and proclaim the salvation of God to them.

Reflection

Why are these truths as important today as they were years ago? Have you asked God to make you holy? To increase the holiness of local church leaders? Why or why not?

The Purpose of Prayer

---

*"The eyes of the LORD are on the righteous,
and His ears are open to their cry."*

PSALM 34:15

Prayer is a sacred, princely privilege. Prayer is a duty, an obligation most binding and most imperative, which should hold us to it. But prayer is more than a privilege, more than a duty. It is a means, an instrument, a condition. Not to pray is to lose much more than to fail in the exercise and enjoyment of a high or sweet privilege. Not to pray is to fail along lines far more important than even the violation of an obligation.

Prayer is the appointed condition of getting God's aid. This aid is as manifold and limitless as God's ability, and as varied and exhaustless is this aid as man's need. Prayer is the avenue through which God supplies man's wants. Prayer is the channel through which all good flows from God to man.

Reflection

Do you tend to view prayer as a duty, an obligation? If so, why? What does the author mean when he says "prayer is more than a privilege"?

God's Cure for Anxiety

*"Later [Jesus] appeared to the eleven as they sat at the table;
and He rebuked their unbelief and hardness of heart."*

MARK 16:14

A simple, confiding faith, casting its burden on the Lord each hour of the day, will dissipate fear, drive away misgivings, and deliver from doubt. As the apostle Paul wrote, "Be anxious for nothing, but in everything by prayer and supplication, with thanksgiving, let your requests be made known to God" (Phil. 4:6). This is the divine cure for all fear, anxiety, and undue concern of soul, all of which are closely related to doubt and unbelief. This is the divine prescription for securing the peace that passes all understanding and keeps the heart and mind in quietness and peace.

All of us need to heed the caution given in Hebrews: "Beware, brethren, lest there be in any of you an evil heart of unbelief in departing from the living God" (3:12). We need to guard against unbelief as we would against an enemy. Faith needs to be cultivated. Faith is increased by exercise, by being put to use. It is nourished by deep trials, "that the genuineness of your faith, being much more precious than gold that perishes, though it is tested by fire, may be found to praise, honor, and glory at the revelation of Jesus Christ" (1 Peter 1:7). Cast your burdens on the Lord and, by faith, know that He will intervene.

Reflection

How strong is your belief that God will bring you through difficulties and help you deal with problems? In what ways might doubts about God and His promises be impacting your life?

God Still Answers Prayers

"I will praise You, for You have answered me."
PSALM 118:21

God has not confined Himself to ancient biblical days in showing what can be done through prayer. In modern times also He is seen to be the same prayer-hearing God as in times past. Religious biography and church history furnish us with many noble examples and striking illustrations of prayer— its necessity, its worth and its fruits—all tending to the encouragement of the faith of God's saints and all urging them on to more and better praying.

God extends far beyond Old and New Testament times in employing praying people as His agents in furthering His cause on earth, and He has placed Himself under obligation to answer their prayers just as much as He did the saints of old. Be assured, God answers prayer now just as He has done throughout history.

Reflection

What happens if we stop expecting God to answer our prayers? Do you really believe God desires to answer your prayers as He answered the prayers of ancient King David? Why or why not?

Growing through Suffering

"And He said, 'Abba, Father, all things are possible for You. Take this cup away from Me; nevertheless, not what I will, but what You will.'"

MARK 14:36

When the sorrow and desolation of Gethsemane fall in heaviest gloom on us, we ought to submit patiently and tearfully, without tremor or doubt, to the cup pressed by the Father's hand to our lips. "Not what I will, but what you will," our broken hearts will say. In God's own way, mysterious to us, that cup has in its bitterest dregs, as it had for the Son of God, the gem and gold of perfection. We are to be put into the crucible to be refined. Christ was made perfect in Gethsemane, not by the prayer but by the suffering. "For it was fitting for Him ... to make the captain of their salvation perfect through sufferings" (Heb. 2:10). The cup could not pass because the suffering had to go on and yield its fruit of perfection.

Through many an hour of darkness and hell's power, through many a deep conflict with the prince of this world, by drinking many bitter cups we are to be made perfect. To cry out against the searching flame of the crucible of the Father's painful processes is natural and is not sin—so long as there is submission to God's will and devotion to His glory.

If our hearts are true to God, we may plead with Him about His way and seek relief from His painful processes. We can cry out in the crucible against the flame that purifies and perfects us. God allows this, hears this, and answers this, not by taking us out of the crucible, but by sending more than an angel to strengthen us.

Reflection

How do you tend to respond when God allows you to suffer? Looking back on your life so far, what has suffering taught you about yourself and God?

Be Devoted to God Every Day

*"Therefore, whether you eat or drink, or whatever you do,
do all to the glory of God."*

1 CORINTHIANS 10:31

Devotion is the spirit of reverence, of awe, of godly fear. It is a state of heart that appears before God in prayer and worship. Devotion dwells in the realm of quietness and is still before God. It is serious, thoughtful, meditative.

This is a busy age, bustling and active, and this bustling spirit has invaded the church of God. Its religious performances are many. The church works at religion with the order, precision, and force of real machinery. But too often it works with the heartlessness of the machine. There is much of the treadmill movement in our ceaseless routine of religious doings. We pray without praying. We sing without singing with the Spirit and the understanding. We have music without the praise of God being in it. We go to church by habit and come home all too gladly when the benediction is pronounced.

We need to put the spirit of devotion into Monday's business as well as in Sunday's worship. The spirit of devotion puts God into all things. It puts God not merely in our praying and churchgoing, but into all the concerns of life. The spirit of devotion makes the common things of earth sacred and the little things great. With this spirit of devotion, we go to business on Monday directed by the same influences and inspired by the same influences by which we went to church on Sunday. The spirit of devotion makes a Sabbath out of Saturday and transforms the shop and the office into a temple of God.

Reflection

What can you do to bring the spirit of devotion into all of your days—your work, your relationships, your prayers?

Instruments of Christ's Power

"The effective, fervent prayer of a righteous man avails much."
JAMES 5:16

The fortunes of the kingdom of Jesus Christ are not made by the feebleness of its foes. They are strong and bitter; they always have been and always will be. But mighty prayer is the one great spiritual force that will enable the Lord Jesus Christ to enter into full possession of His kingdom and secure for Him the heathen as His inheritance and the uttermost part of the earth for His possession.

It is prayer that will enable Him to break His foes with a rod of iron, that will make these foes tremble in their pride and power. For they are but frail clay vessels to be broken in pieces by one stroke of His hand. A person who can pray is the mightiest instrument Christ has in this world. A praying church is stronger than all the gates of hell.

Reflection

If prayer is mighty powerful in the spiritual battle, why don't more Christians pray fervently? Why do you think Jesus depends so much on the prayers of His church?

Hope Rests in the Resurrection

"Blessed be the God and Father of our Lord Jesus Christ, who according to His abundant mercy has begotten us again to a living hope through the resurrection of Jesus Christ from the dead, to an inheritance incorruptible and undefiled and that does not fade away, reserved in heaven for you."

1 PETER 1:3–4

The resurrection of Jesus Christ is the birth of a new, glorious, immortal life on the realms of the midnight of death, the rising of the new sun on the terrors of darkness and night. It is the opening of a bright and noble highway to heaven where everything had been closed and sealed and every hope had withered.

The resurrection of Christ not only lifts darkness and dread from the tomb, but also spans the abyss that separates us from our loved dead and puts into us the strength and hope of a glorious reunion in the very face of a most painful, disastrous, and despairing separation. Hope throws its rich luster over the night of the tomb and thrills with deathless joy the heart in which the resurrection of Jesus has been realized.

Reflection

How much hope does Jesus' resurrection, and the resurrection promised to all believers, bring to you? How does the Bible's resurrection hope aid us in facing the deaths of our loved ones who received Jesus as their Lord and Savior?

The Source of Perfect Peace

"You will keep him in perfect peace, whose mind is stayed on You."
ISAIAH 26:3

The spirit of consecration is the spirit of prayer. The law of consecration is the law of prayer. Both laws work in perfect harmony without the slightest dissonance or discord. Consecration is the practical expression of true prayer. People who are consecrated are known by their praying habits. Consecration thus expresses itself in prayer. The person who is not interested in prayer has no interest in consecration. Prayer creates an interest in consecration, then prayer brings one into a state of heart where consecration is a subject of delight, bringing joy of heart, satisfaction of soul, and contentment of spirit.

The consecrated person is the happiest person. There is no friction whatever between the person who is fully given over to God and the will of God. There is perfect harmony between the will of such a person and God and His will. And the two wills being in perfect accord brings rest of soul, absence of friction, and the presence of perfect peace.

Reflection

What is the relationship between personal consecration to God and prayer? In what ways do they complement one another?

Be Wary of Wealth

*"Beware that you do not forget the L*ORD *your God ... lest—when you have eaten and are full, and have built beautiful houses and dwell in them; and when your herds and your flocks multiply, and your silver and your gold are multiplied ... then you say in your heart, 'My power and the might of my hand have gained me this wealth.'"*

DEUTERONOMY 8:11–13, 17

Material prosperity is not the infallible sign of spiritual prosperity. The former may exist while the latter is significantly absent. Material accumulation easily blinds the eyes of Christians, so much so that they will make it a substitute for spiritual progress. How great is the need to watch at that point!

The seasons of material prosperity are rarely seasons of spiritual advance, either to the individual or the church. It is so easy to lose sight of God when goods increase. It is so easy to lean on human agencies and cease praying and relying on God when material prosperity comes.

Reflection

Do you agree that times of material prosperity are rarely times of spiritual advance? What effect has material prosperity had on you and/or other people around you?

Busyness May Mask Problems

"As you therefore have received Christ Jesus the Lord, so walk in Him, rooted and built up in Him and established in the faith."

COLOSSIANS 2:6–7

Activity is not strength. Work is not zeal. Moving about is not devotion. In fact, activity often is the unrecognized symptom of spiritual weakness. It may be hurtful to piety when made the substitute for real devotion in worship. The colt is much more active than its mother, but it is she that pulls the load without noise, bluster, or show. The child is more active than the father, who may be bearing the rule and burdens of an empire on his heart and shoulders. Enthusiasm is more active than faith, though it cannot remove mountains or call into action any omnipotent forces that faith can command.

A feeble, lively, showy religious activity may spring from many causes. There is much running around, much stirring about, much going here and there in present-day church life— but the spirit of genuine, heartfelt devotion is strangely lacking. If there is real spiritual life, productive and fruitful activity will spring from it. But it is an activity springing from strength and not from weakness. It is an activity that has roots, deep and strong.

Reflection

What can happen when a person is busily involved in "religious" activities yet is not deeply rooted in Jesus? What can you do to "grow deeper roots"?

What Praying People Desire

*"If two of you agree on earth concerning anything that they ask,
it will be done for them by My Father in heaven."*

MATTHEW 18:19

M any Christians are stagnant because they have no pat-
tern and plan by which character and conduct are
shaped. They just move on aimlessly, their minds in a cloudy
state, no clear direction in view, no point in sight, no standard after which they are striving. No magnet is there to fill
their eyes, quicken their steps, and draw them and keep
them steady.

All this vague idea of religion grows out of loose notions
about prayer. Prayer helps to make the standard of religion
clear and definite. Prayer aids in placing the standard high.
Praying people are those who have something definite in view.
In fact, prayer itself is a very definite thing, aims at something
specific, and has a mark at which it aims. Prayer aims at the
most definite, highest, and sweetest religious experience.

Praying people want all that God has in store for them.
They are not satisfied with anything like a low religious life—
superficial, vague, and indefinite. Praying people are not only
after a "deeper work of grace"; they want the very *deepest* work
of grace possible and promised. They are not after being saved
from some sin, but saved from all sin, both inward and outward. They are after not only deliverance from sinning, but

from sin itself—its being, its power, and its pollution. They are after holiness of heart and life.

Reflection

Toward what or whom are you advancing? In what ways does prayer affect standards of conduct and character?

A Key to God's Blessings

"Now to Him who is able to do exceedingly abundantly above all that we ask or think...."

EPHESIANS 3:20

Why do Christians sometimes complain that their lives are not full, that they feel incomplete, that something is missing? Why do so many lack the richness and fullness, the depth and breadth, spoke of in the Bible? The answer is simply this: They have not given themselves fully and completely to God.

God gives Himself and His riches unreservedly to those who have unreservedly committed themselves to Him. The man who gives all to God will receive all from God. Having given all to God, he can claim all that God has for him.

Reflection

Why does God demand our full commitment? What does it mean specifically to give ourselves fully and completely to God?

Trouble Is a Teacher

*"Man who is born of woman is of
few days and full of trouble."*

JOB 14:1

Trouble is common to man. There is no exception in any age, climate, or station. Rich and poor alike, the learned and the ignorant, one and all are partakers of this sad and painful inheritance of the fall of man.

To expect nothing but sunshine and look only for ease, pleasure, and flowers is an entirely false view of life. Those who anticipate a trouble-free life are sorely disappointed and surprised when difficulties descend upon them. These people do not understand the ways of God and know little of His disciplinary dealings with His children.

Trouble is under the control of almighty God and is one of His most efficient agents in fulfilling His purposes and perfecting His saints. God's hand is in every problem that breaks into people's lives. Not that He directly and arbitrarily orders every unpleasant experience. Not that He is personally responsible for every painful and afflicting thing that comes into the lives of His people. But no trouble is ever turned loose in this world and comes into the life of saint or sinner without divine permission. God allows it to exist and do its painful work with God's hand in it or on it, carrying out His gracious designs of redemption.

All things are under divine control. Trouble is neither above God nor beyond His control. It is not something in life independent of God. No matter from what source it springs, God is sufficiently wise and able to lay His hand on it without assuming responsibility for its origin and work it into His plans and purposes concerning the highest welfare of His saints.

Reflection

How is this perspective on trouble different from others you may have heard? How has God used trouble to shape your life? Are you able to trust that He is using your trouble in a divine way, or do you rebel against this truth?

What Your Life Says to Others

"By their fruits you will know them."
MATTHEW 7:20

In carrying on His great mission in the world, God works through human agents. He works through His church collectively and through His people individually. In order to be effective agents, they must each be "a vessel for honor, sanctified and useful for the Master, prepared for every good work" (2 Tim. 2:21). God works most effectively through holy men. His work makes progress in the hands of devout, dutiful, and diligent people.

Peter tells us that husbands who might not be reached by the Word of God might be won by the conversation of their wives. It is those who are "blameless and harmless, children of God" who can hold forth the word of life "in the midst of a crooked and perverse generation" (Phil. 2:15). The world judges religion not by what the Bible says, but by how Christians live. Christians are the Bible that sinners read. These are the Epistles to be read by all men.

Reflection

As people "read the book" of your daily life, what do they learn about God? In what ways do your actions and attitudes accurately reflect God's truth? In what ways do you need to change and improve?

Answered Prayer Assures Us of God's Care

"By awesome deeds in righteousness You will answer us, O God of our salvation."

PSALM 65:5

God's children pray. They rest in Him for all things. They ask Him for all things—for everything. The faith of the child in the Father is manifested by the child's asking. It is the answer to prayer that convinces people not only that there is a God, but that He is a God who concerns Himself about people and the dealings of this world. Answered prayer brings God near and assures people of His being.

The possibilities of prayer are found in God's limitless promise, the willingness and the power of God to answer prayer—to answer all prayer and to supply fully the boundless need of mankind. None are so needy and wanting as we are; none are so able and anxious to supply any and every need as God.

Reflection

To what extent do you give God the opportunity to concern Himself with *your* life and the lives of your loved ones? How has God responded to your prayers recently?

Discerning the Will of God

"Be transformed by the renewing of your mind, that you may prove what is that good and acceptable and perfect will of God."

ROMANS 12:2

It may be asked how we are to know what God's will is. The answer is by studying His Word, by hiding it in our hearts, and by letting the Word dwell in us richly. As the psalmist said, "The entrance of Your words gives light" (119:130).

To know God's will, we must be filled with God's Spirit, who makes intercession for the saints. To be filled with God's Spirit, to be filled with God's Word, is to know God's will. It is to be put in such a frame of mind, to be found in such a state of heart, as will enable us to read and interpret correctly God's purposes. Such filling of the heart, with the Word and the Holy Spirit, gives us insight into the Father's will, enables us to rightly discern His will, and puts within us a disposition of mind and heart to make it the guide and compass of our lives.

Epaphras prayed that the Colossians might stand "perfect and complete in all the will of God" (4:12). This is positive proof that not only may we know God's will, but we may know all of God's will. And not only may we know all of God's will, we may do all of God's will. We may, moreover, do all of God's will with a settled habit of conduct, not occasionally or by mere impulse. Knowing and doing the will of God can become not the exception but the rule of our lives.

Reflection

How highly do you value knowing the will of God? Does the time you spend in the Bible reflect that?

Pray Specifically

"I will cry out to God Most High, to God who performs all things for me."
PSALM 57:2

Prayer is no little thing, no small matter or selfish indulgence. It does not concern the petty interests of one person. The littlest prayer broadens out by the will of God until it touches all words, conserves all interests, and enhances man's greatest wealth and God's greatest good. God is so concerned that men pray that He has promised to answer prayer. He has not promised to do something general if we pray, but He has promised to do the very thing for which we pray.

Prayer is an ardent and believing cry to God for some specific thing. God's rule is to answer by giving the specific thing asked for. With it may come much of other gifts and graces. Strength, serenity, sweetness, and faith may come as the bearers of the gifts. But even they come because God hears and answers prayer.

God is concerned most of all with the particulars of our lives, the details and the fine points. When approaching Him, let us dwell not on generalities but on specifics, that He may answer us in clear, distinct, and specific ways.

Reflection

Why is it best to pray about specific needs rather than generalities? Why is it easy to utter only vague and imprecise kinds of prayers?

Is Adversity Hardening or Softening You?

"He shall call upon Me, and I will answer him; I will be with him in trouble; I will deliver him and honor him."

PSALM 91:15

Prayer during times of trouble tends to bring the spirit into perfect subjection to God's will, to cause the will to be conformed to God's will, saves from all complaining over our lot, and delivers from everything like a rebellious attitude. Prayer sanctifies trouble to our highest good. Prayer so prepares the heart that it softens under God's disciplining hand. Prayer places us where God can bring to us the greatest good, spiritual and eternal.

The result of trouble is always good in the mind of God. If trouble fails in its mission, it is either because of prayerlessness or unbelief, or both. Being in harmony with God in the dispensations of His providence always makes trouble a blessing. The good or evil of trouble is always determined by the spirit in which it is received. Adversity proves to be a blessing or a curse, according to how we receive and treat it. Hardship either softens or hardens us. It either draws us to prayer and God, or it drives us from God and from the prayer closet. The same sun softens the wax and hardens the clay. The same sun melts the ice and dries out the earth's moisture.

Reflection

In what spirit do you typically receive adversity? How might you better appropriate God's promises in the Bible during difficult times?

Seek Christlike Compassion

"When He saw the multitudes, He was moved with compassion for them."
MATTHEW 9:36

Compassion is moved at the sight of sin, sorrow, and suffering. It stands at the other extreme to indifference to other people's wants and woes. It is far removed from insensibility and hardness of heart in the midst of want, trouble, and wretchedness.

A certain compassion belongs to the natural man and expends its force in simple gifts to those in need, not to be despised. But spiritual compassion—the kind born in a renewed heart—is deeper, broader, and more loving. This sort of compassion goes beyond the relief of mere bodily wants and says, "Be warm, be clothed." Hard-hearted is he, and far from being Christlike, who sees the multitudes and is unmoved at the sight of their sad state, unhappiness, and peril.

Compassion may not always move people but is always moved toward people. Compassion may not always turn people to God, but it will and does turn God to people. And where it is most helpless to relieve the needs of others, it can at least break out into prayer to God for others.

Reflection

How compassionate are you? In what ways might you demonstrate Christlike compassion to people in your community?

The Power of Believing Prayer

"I trust in Your word."
PSALM 119:42

God's promises are altogether too large to be mastered by inconsistent and random praying. When we examine ourselves, all too often we discover that our praying does not rise to the demands of the situation, being so limited that it is little more than a mere oasis amid the waste and desert of the world's sin. Recall the words of our Lord: "Most assuredly, I say to you, he who believes in Me, the works that I do he will do also; and greater works than these he will do, because I go to My Father" (John 14:12). Who of us, in our praying, measures up to this awesome promise?

How comprehensive this promise is—how far-reaching, how all-embracing! How much is here for the glory of God and for the good of man! How much is here for the manifestation of Christ's enthroned power. How much is here for the reward of abundant faith! And how great and gracious are the results that can be made to accrue from the exercise of commensurate, believing prayer!

Reflection

What role does your faith have in receiving blessings from God through prayer? How much do you *really* trust God and His promises in the Bible as you face various situations.

Don't Miss Out on God's Work

*"The shepherds have become dull-hearted, and have not sought
the LORD; therefore they shall not prosper, and
all their flocks shall be scattered."*

JEREMIAH 10:21

When we say that prayer "puts God to work," it is simply to say that man has it in his power by prayer to move God to work in His own way among men, in which way He would not work if prayer was not made. Thus while prayer moves God to work, at the same time He puts prayer to work. As God has ordained prayer, and as prayer has no existence separate from men, then logically prayer is the one force that puts God to work in earth's affairs.

Then, by the same token, prayerlessness rules God out of the world's dealings and fails to activate His workings. Prayerlessness excludes God from everything concerning men and leaves man on earth the mere creature of circumstances, at the mercy of blind fate or without help of any kind from God. It leaves man in this world—with its tremendous responsibilities, difficult problems, sorrows, burdens, and afflictions—without any God at all. In reality the denial of prayer is a denial of God Himself because He and prayer are so inseparable that they can never be divorced.

Reflection

What is "prayerlessness," and why do you think it is rampant among many Christians today? In what ways do you need God to work in your life right now?

Called to Watchfulness

"Be sober, be vigilant; because your adversary the devil walks about like a roaring lion, seeking whom he may devour."

1 Peter 5:8

It's a fact that the Devil never falls asleep. He is always walking about, "seeking whom he may devour." Just as a shepherd must never be careless and unwatchful lest the wolf devour his sheep, so the Christian soldier must always have his eyes wide open. The inseparable companions and safeguards of prayer are vigilance, watchfulness, and a mounted guard. In writing to the Colossians, Paul brackets these inseparable qualities together: "Continue earnestly in prayer," he enjoins, "being vigilant in it with thanksgiving" (4:2).

The entire life of a Christian soldier—its being, intention, implication, and action—are all dependent on its being a life of prayer. Without prayer, no matter what else he has, the Christian soldier will be feeble, ineffective, and make him an easy prey for his spiritual enemies.

When will Christians more thoroughly learn the twofold lesson that they are called to a great warfare and that victory is achieved only through unsleeping watchfulness and unceasing prayer? God's church is a militant host. Its warfare is with unseen forces of evil. God's people constitute an army fighting to establish His kingdom on the earth. Their aim is to destroy the sovereignty of Satan, and over its ruins erect the kingdom of God.

Reflection

Are you engaged in the spiritual battle—or primarily observing from the sidelines? What might God want to accomplish through you in the spiritual battle raging all around you?

Two Vital Questions

"We desire that ... you do not become sluggish, but imitate those who through faith and patience inherit the promises."

HEBREWS 6:11–12

Faith grows by reading and meditating on the Word of God. Most and best of all, faith thrives in an atmosphere of prayer. It would be well if all of us were to stop and ask ourselves, *Have I real faith in God—faith that keeps me in perfect peace concerning the things of earth and heaven?* This is the most important question a man can propound and expect to be answered. And there is another question, closely related to it in significance and importance: *Do I really pray to God so that He hears me and answers my prayers—so that I receive directly from Him the things I ask of Him?*

For the Christian who desires an ever-closer walk with God and to be mighty in His service, these two questions must be regularly pondered.

Reflection

How would you respond to these two vital questions? Ask God to show you how your faith might be deepened and your prayer life enriched.

Prayer Generates Love for the Church

---

*"I write so that you may know how you ought to conduct yourself
in the house of God, which is the church of the living God,
the pillar and ground of the truth."*

1 TIMOTHY 3:15

Just as prayer generates a love for the Scriptures and sets people to reading the Bible, so prayer causes men and women to visit the house of God to hear the Scriptures expounded. Churchgoing is closely connected with the Bible, not so much because the Bible cautions us against "forsaking the assembling of ourselves together, as is the manner of some" (Heb. 10:25), but because in God's house His chosen minister declares the Word to dying people, explains the Scriptures, and emphasizes their teachings upon his hearers. Prayer generates a resolve, in those who practice it, not to forsake the house of God.

Prayer generates a churchgoing conscience, a church-loving heart, and a church-supporting spirit. It is the praying people who make it a matter of conscience to attend the preaching of the Word, who delight in its reading and exposition, who support it with their influence and their means. Prayer exalts the Word of God and gives it preeminence in the estimation of those who faithfully and wholeheartedly call on the name of the Lord.

Reflection

How would you describe the connection between prayer and love for church? What effect has prayer had on your attitudes toward, and participation in, regular meetings of believers where the Bible is taught?

Beware of "Spiritual Adultery"

"Adulterers and adulteresses! Do you not know that friendship with the world is enmity with God? Whoever therefore wants to be a friend of the world makes himself an enemy of God."

JAMES 4:4

Nothing is more explicit than this. Nothing is more commanding, authoritative, and exacting. "Do not love the world" (1 John 2:15). Nothing is more offensive to God, more abominable, and in violation of the most sacred relationship with the Father. Friendship with the world is God's greatest enemy as it represents a kind of "spiritual adultery."

The world is one of the enemies that must be fought and conquered on the way to heaven. "The world" includes the whole mass of people alienated from God and therefore hostile to the cause of Christ. It involves worldly matters, the whole circle of earthly goods, endowments, riches, advantages, pleasures, and pursuits that lure us away from God. In essence, "the world" includes anything that would distract or divide us from God and His will.

In that fatal hour when man fell from his allegiance and devotion to God, he carried the world with him in his rebellion against God. Man was the world's lord, and it fell with its lord. This is the reason for its full influence, its malignant rivalry, and its intense opposition to heaven. The Devil has his kingdom here. He clothes it with all beauty and seductive power as heaven's rival. Heaven's trinity of foes are the world, the flesh, and the Devil. The flesh wars with the spirit simply because the Devil inflames its desires. The world is not simply Satan's ally, but also his instrument and agent. It represents him with the most servile and complete loyalty.

Reflection

Which aspects of "the world" most tempt you? How does any form of "spiritual adultery" affect a believer's day-to-day relationship with God? Why?

Making Unholy Hearts Holy

*"As He who called you is holy, you also be holy in all your
conduct, because it is written, 'Be holy, for I am holy.'"*

1 PETER 1:15–16

God is governing this world, with its intelligent beings, for His glory and their good. What, then, is God's work in this world? Rather, what is the end He seeks in His great work? It is nothing short of holiness of heart and life in the children of fallen Adam. Man is a fallen creature, born with an evil nature, with an evil bent, unholy propensities, and sinful desires.

God's entire plan is to take hold of fallen man and seek to change him and make him holy. God's work is to make holy men out of unholy men. This is the very end of Christ coming into the world: "For this purpose the Son of God was manifested, that He might destroy the works of the devil" (1 John 3:8).

God is holy in nature and in all His ways, and He wants to make man like Himself. This is being Christlike. This is following Jesus Christ. This is the aim of all Christian effort. This is the earnest, heartfelt desire of every truly regenerated soul. This is what is to be constantly and earnestly prayed for. It is that we may be made holy. Not that we must make ourselves holy, but we must be cleansed from all sin by Christ's precious atoning blood and be made holy by the Holy Spirit's direct agency. Not that we are to *do* holy things, but rather to *be* holy people. *Being* must precede *doing*. First obtain a holy heart, then live a holy life. For this high and gracious end, God has made the most ample provisions in the atoning work of our Lord and through the Holy Spirit's agency.

Reflection

How is holiness developed, and why does the desire for holiness need to start within the heart? What are the key differences between *being* and *doing?*

What Makes Prayer Potent?

"May the God of hope fill you with all joy and peace in believing, that you may abound in hope by the power of the Holy Spirit."

ROMANS 15:13

Would we pray efficiently and mightily? Then the Holy Spirit must work in us efficiently and mightily. Paul asserts this principle, which applies to every believer: "To this end I also labor, striving according to His working which works in me mightily" (Col. 1:29).

All labor for Christ that does not spring from the Holy Spirit working in us is worthless and vain. Our prayers and activities are so feeble and fruitless because He has not worked in us and cannot work through us by the Spirit's power. Would you pray with mighty results? Seek the mighty workings of the Holy Spirit in your own spirit.

Reflection

How mighty are the workings of the Holy Spirit in your life? Are you completely committed to allowing Him to work gloriously within you?

Wholehearted Devotion

"Who then is willing to consecrate himself this day to the Lord?"

1 Chronicles 29:5

Consecration is the voluntary, determined dedication of oneself to God, an offering definitely made without any reservation whatsoever. It is the setting apart of all we are, all we have, and all we expect to have or be, to God first of all. It is not so much the giving of ourselves to the church, or the mere engaging in some aspect of church work. Almighty God is in view, and He is the end of all consecration. Consecration has a sacred nature. It is devoted to holy ends. It is voluntarily placing oneself in God's hands to be used sacredly, with sanctifying ends in view.

Consecration is not so much setting oneself apart from sinful things and wicked ends. Rather, it is the separation from worldly, secular, and even legitimate things—if they come in conflict with God's plans—to holy uses. It is to devote all we have to God for His specific use. It is a separation from things questionable, or even legitimate, when the choice is to be made between the things of this life and the claims of God.

The consecration that meets God's demands and that He accepts is to be full, complete, with nothing held back. It cannot be partial, any more than a whole burnt offering during Old Testament times could have been partial. The whole animal had to be offered in sacrifice. To reserve any part of the animal would have seriously invalidated the offering. So, to make a half-hearted, partial consecration is to make no consecration at all and fail utterly in securing divine acceptance.

Reflection

What types of things hold believers back from full and complete consecration to God? What might God be saying to you through this reading about *your* devotion to Him?

Faith and Prayer Are Intertwined

*"Without faith it is impossible to please Him, for he who comes
to God must believe that He is, and that He is a rewarder
of those who diligently seek Him."*

HEBREWS 11:6

Faith opens the way for prayer to approach God. But it does more. Faith accompanies prayer at every step it takes. It is prayer's inseparable companion and, when requests are made to God, faith turns the asking into obtaining. What's more, faith follows prayer, since the spiritual life into which a believer is led by prayer is a life of faith.

Faith makes prayer strong and gives it patience to wait on God. Faith believes that God is a rewarder. No truth is more clearly revealed in the Scriptures than this, while none is more encouraging. Faith is narrowed down to one particular thing: It does not believe that God will reward everybody, nor that He is a rewarder of all who pray, but that He is a rewarder of those who *diligently seek Him*. Faith rests its care on diligence in prayer and gives assurance to diligent seekers after God. They alone are richly rewarded when they pray.

We need constantly to be reminded that faith is the one inseparable condition of successful praying. There are other considerations entering into the exercise, but faith is the final, indispensable condition of true praying.

Reflection

What is involved in "diligent" seeking? What role does faith play in the exercise of prayer?

The Bible: Our Only Sure Standard

"We dare not class ourselves or compare ourselves with those who commend themselves. But they, measuring themselves by themselves, and comparing themselves among themselves, are not wise."

2 CORINTHIANS 10:12

The Scriptures alone make the standard of life and experience. When we make our own standard, there is delusion and falsity for our desires, convenience and pleasure form the rule, and that is always a fleshly, low rule. From it, all the fundamental principles of a Christly religion are left out. Whatever standard of religion makes in it provision for the flesh is unscriptural and hurtful.

Nor will it do to leave it to others to establish the standard of religion for us. When we allow others to make our standard of religion, it is generally deficient because in imitation, defects are transferred to the imitator more readily than virtues, and a second edition of a man is marred by its defects.

The most serious damage in determining what religion is by what others say is in allowing current opinion—whatever happens to be the accepted norm or measure—to shape our religious opinions and characters. Adoniram Judson once wrote to a friend, "Let me beg you not to rest contented with the commonplace religion that is now so prevalent."

Commonplace religion is pleasing to flesh and blood. There is no self-denial in it, no cross-bearing, and no self-crucifixion. It is good enough for our neighbors. Why should we be set apart and above reproach? Others are living on a low plane, on a compromising level, living as the world lives. Why should we be peculiar, zealous of good works? Why should we fight to win heaven while so many are sailing there on "flowery beds of ease"?

Why? Because it is God's standard at which we are to aim and not man's.

Reflection

What happens when Christians allow other people and current opinions, rather than the Bible, to determine their standards? Do you know the Bible well enough to really make it your gauge for godly living?

Church Discipline Is Essential

"Brethren, if a man is overtaken in any trespass, you who are spiritual restore such a one in a spirit of gentleness, considering yourself lest you also be tempted."

GALATIANS 6:1

The work of the church is not just to seek members but to watch over and guard them after they have entered the church. And if any are overtaken by sin, they must be sought out. If they cannot be cured of their faults, excision must take place.

As good a church as that at Thessalonica needed instruction and caution on this matter of looking after disorderly persons. So we hear Paul saying to them, "But we command you, brethren, in the name of our Lord Jesus Christ, that you withdraw from every brother who walks disorderly" (2 Thess. 3:6). Mind you, it is not the mere presence of disorderly persons in a church that merits God's displeasure. It is when they are tolerated under the mistaken plea of "bearing with them," and no steps are taken either to cure them of their evil practices or exclude them from the church's fellowship. This glaring neglect on the part of the church of its wayward members is but a sad sign of a lack of praying because a praying church—given to mutual praying, agreement praying—is keen to discern when a brother is overtaken in a fault and seeks either to restore him or cut him off if he is incorrigible.

Does that seem a harsh course? Then our Lord was guilty of harshness. For He said, "If he refuses even to hear the church, let him be to you like a heathen and a tax collector" (Matt. 18:17). No more is this harshness than is the act of the skillful surgeon, who sees the whole body and its members endangered by a gangrenous limb and severs it from the body for the good of the whole. What seems harshness is obedience to God—and welfare for the church.

Reflection

Why must the church discipline "disorderly" members? How has the name of Jesus been shamed because this discipline did not occur?

Prayer and the Assurance of Heaven

"Our citizenship is in heaven, from which we also eagerly wait for the Savior, the Lord Jesus Christ."

PHILIPPIANS 3:20

The Scriptures furnish great incentives to pray. The presence of Christ in heaven, the preparation for His saints He is making there, and the assurance that He will come again to receive them—all of this helps the weariness of praying, strengthens its resolves, and sweetens its arduous toil. These are the star of hope to prayer, the wiping away of its tears, the putting of the aroma of heaven into the bitterness of its cry.

The spirit of a pilgrim greatly facilitates praying. An earthbound spirit cannot pray. In such a heart, the flame of spiritual desire has either gone out or smolders in faintest glow. The wings of its faith are clipped, its tongue is silenced. But those who in unswerving faith and unceasing prayer wait continually on the Lord renew their strength, mount up with wings as eagles, run and are not weary, and walk and do not faint.

Reflection

How often do you think about heaven and what believers will experience there? What do you think is the relationship between waiting continually on the Lord and God's promises concerning heaven?

What the Church Needs Today

*"We will give ourselves continually to prayer and
to the ministry of the word."*

ACTS 6:4

Schools, colleges, and education cannot be regarded as being leaders in carrying forward the work of God's kingdom in the world. They have neither the right, the will, nor the power to do the work. This is to be accomplished by the preached Word, delivered in the power of the Holy Spirit sent down from heaven, sown with prayerful hands, and watered with the tears of praying hearts.

People are essential to the great work of soul saving, and people must go. It is no angelic or impersonal force that is needed. Human hearts baptized with the spirit of prayer must bear the burden of this message, and human tongues on fire as the result of earnest, persistent prayer must declare the Word of God to dying men.

The church today needs praying people to execute her solemn and pressing responsibility to meet the fearful crisis that is facing her. The crying need of the times is for God-fearing people, praying people, Holy Spirit people, people who will submit all things unto the cross of Christ. The people who are so greatly needed in this age of the church are those who have learned the business of praying—learned it on their knees, learned it in the need and agony of their own hearts.

Reflection

What sacrifices might God want you to make to further His kingdom? Ask God to show you ways in which you can grow closer to Him and in the knowledge of Jesus Christ.

The Spirit of Missions

"Go into all the world and preach the gospel to every creature."

MARK 16:15

The Spirit of Jesus Christ is the spirit of missions. His promise and advent composed the first missionary movement. The missionary spirit is not simply a phase of the gospel, not a mere feature of the plan of salvation, but is its very spirit and life. The missionary movement is the church of Jesus Christ marching in militant array, with the goal of possessing the whole world of mankind for Christ.

Whoever is touched by the Spirit of God is fired by the missionary spirit. An antimissionary Christian is a contradiction in terms. We might say that it would be impossible to be an antimissionary Christian because of the impossibility for the divine and human forces to put people in such a state as not to align them with the missionary cause. Missionary impulse is the heartbeat of our Lord Jesus Christ, sending His vital forces through the whole body of the church. The spiritual life of God's people rises or falls with the force of those heartbeats. When these life forces cease, then death ensues. So, antimissionary churches are dead churches, just as antimissionary Christians are dead Christians.

Reflection

What excuses do many Christians give for not sharing the life and truth of Jesus with other people? Do you agree that an "antimissionary" church is a dead church? Why or why not?

The Importance of Spiritual Faith

*"When the Son of Man comes, will He really
find faith on the earth?"*

LUKE 18:8

Is faith growing or declining as the years go by? Does faith stand strong and firm these days, as iniquity abounds and the love of many people grows cold? Does faith maintain its hold, as religion tends to become a mere formality and worldliness increasingly prevails? This question of our Lord may, with great appropriateness, be ours. "When the Son of Man comes, will He really find faith on the earth?" We believe that He will, and it is our responsibility in this day, to see to it that the lamp of faith is trimmed and burning.

Faith is the foundation of Christian character and the security of the soul. When Jesus was anticipating Peter's denial and cautioning him against it, He said to His disciple: "Simon, Simon! Indeed, Satan has asked for you, that he may sift you as wheat. But I have prayed for you, that your faith should not fail" (Luke 22:31–32).

Our Lord was declaring a central truth. It was Peter's faith He was seeking to guard, for He well knew that when faith is broken down the foundations of spiritual life give way, and the entire structure of religious experience falls. It was Peter's faith that needed guarding.

Reflection

Has your faith increased—or decreased—during recent years? Why? How has your faith impacted your life and the lives of people around you?

Trust: The Outstretched Hand

*"Cause me to hear Your lovingkindness in
the morning, for in You do I trust."*

PSALM 143:8

The center of trust is God. Mountains of difficulties, and all other hindrances to prayer, are moved out of the way by trust. When trust is perfect and without doubt, prayer is simply the outstretched hand ready to receive. Trust perfected is prayer perfected. Trust looks to receive the thing asked for— and gets it. Trust is not a belief that God can bless, that He will bless, but that He *does* bless, here and now.

Trust always operates in the present tense. Hope looks toward the future. Trust looks to the present while hope expects. Trust receives what prayer acquires. So what prayer needs, at all times, is abiding and abundant trust.

Reflection

Is your hand outstretched to God today, ready to receive prayerfully? Why or why not?

Pray for Others' Salvation

---

*"There is one God and one Mediator between God
and men, the Man Christ Jesus."*

1 TIMOTHY 2:5

Jesus Christ—a man, the God-man, the highest illustration of manhood—is the mediator between God and man. Jesus Christ, this divine man, died for all men. His life is but an intercession for all men. His death is but a prayer for all men. On earth Jesus Christ knew no higher law, no holier business, and no diviner life than to plead for men. In heaven, He knows no more royal estate, no higher theme, than to intercede for men. On earth He lived and prayed and died for men. His life, His death, and His exaltation in heaven all plead for men.

Is there any higher work for the disciple to do than what his Lord did? Is there any loftier employment more honorable and divine than to pray for the salvation of others? Can we aspire to any greater mission than to break the slavery that binds them, the hell that holds them, and lift them to immortality and eternal life? Nothing seems so great as the intercession on behalf of others' souls—so let us pray fervently and without fail.

Reflection

How committed are you to interceding on behalf of people who need God? Pray that God will bring people to mind for whom you can pray regularly.

What Faith Is ... and Is Not

"The just shall live by his faith."

HABAKKUK 2:4

Faith is not an abstract belief in God's Word, a mere mental credence, a simple assent of the understanding and will. Nor is faith a passive acceptance of facts, however sacred or thorough. Faith is an operation of God, a divine illumination, a holy energy implanted by God's Word and the Holy Spirit in the human soul.

Faith deals with God and is conscious of God. It deals with the Lord Jesus Christ and sees in Him a Savior. It deals with God's Word and lays hold of the truth. It deals with God's Spirit and is energized and inspired by His holy fire. God is the great objective of faith because faith rests its whole weight on His Word. Faith is not an aimless act of the soul, but a looking toward God and a resting on His promises. Just as love and hope always have an objective, so also has faith. Faith is not believing just *anything;* it is believing God, resting in Him, and trusting His Word.

Faith gives birth to prayer and grows stronger, strikes deeper, and rises higher during the struggles and wrestlings of mighty petitioning. Faith is the substance of things hoped for, the assurance and realization of the saints' inheritance. Faith is humble and persevering. It can wait and pray; it can stay on its knees or lie in the dust. Faith is the one great condition of prayer, and lack of it lies at the root of all poor praying, feeble praying, little praying, and unanswered praying.

Faith's nature and meaning is more demonstrable in what it does than it is by reason of any definition given it. Thus, if we turn to the record of faith given us in that great honor roll, which constitutes Hebrews 11, we see something of the wonderful results of faith.

Reflection

In what ways has your level of faith affected your life, especially your prayer life? Do you agree that faith's nature and meaning is more demonstrable by actions than by definitions? Why or why not?

Removing Obstacles

*"You shall keep My statutes, and perform them:
I am the LORD who sanctifies you."*

LEVITICUS 20:8

If you have an earnest desire to pray well, you must learn how to obey well. If you have a desire to learn to pray, you must have an earnest desire to learn how to do God's will. If you desire to pray to God, you must first have a consuming desire to obey Him. If you would have free access to God in prayer, every obstacle in the nature of sin or disobedience must be removed.

Everywhere in Holy Scripture, God is represented as disapproving of disobedience and condemning sin, and this is as true in the lives of His elect as it is in the lives of sinners. Nowhere does He tolerate sin or excuse disobedience. Always, God ties the emphasis on obedience to His commands. Obedience to them brings blessing; disobedience meets with disaster. This is true in the Word of God from its beginning to its close.

Prayer is obedience. It is founded on the unyielding rock of obedience to God. Only those who obey have the right to pray. Behind the praying must be the doing. It is the constant doing of God's will in daily life that gives prayer its potency.

Reflection

Why do so many people, including Christians, choose to disregard some of God's commands in the Bible? How can you obey God today, and encourage other people to do so, in the face of so many temptations?

Your Divine Helper

"I will pray the Father, and He will give you another Helper,
that He may abide with you forever."

JOHN 14:16

The Holy Spirit is not only the bright lamp of the Christian dispensation—its Teacher and Guide—but is the divine Helper. He is the enabling agent in God's new dispensation of doing. As the pilot takes his stand at the wheel to guide the vessel, so the Holy Spirit takes up His abode in the heart to guide and empower all its efforts. The Holy Spirit executes the whole gospel through the man by His presence and control of the spirit of the man. In the execution of the atoning work of Jesus Christ, in its general and more comprehensive operation, or in its minute and personal application, the Holy Spirit is the one efficient agent, absolute and indispensable.

Only the Holy Spirit can execute the gospel. Only He has the authority to do this royal work. Intellect cannot execute it, neither can learning, eloquence, truth, or even the revealed truth. The marvelous facts of Christ's life told by hearts unanointed by the Holy Spirit will be dry and sterile, or "like a story told by an idiot, full of sound and fury, signifying nothing," as Shakespeare wrote. Only tongues set on fire by the Holy Spirit can witness the saving power of Christ with power to save others.

Reflection

In what ways is the Holy Spirit working in your life? Why is His presence so essential in your life?

Make Your Prayers Big and Bold

"He who did not spare His own Son, but delivered him up for us all, how shall He not with Him also freely give us all things?"

ROMANS 8:32

Almighty God seems to fear we will hesitate to ask largely, apprehensive that we will strain His ability. He declares that He is "able to do exceedingly abundantly above all that we ask or think" (Eph. 3:20). How He charges, commands, and urges us to pray!

God gave us all things in prayer by promise because He had given us all things in His Son. What an astounding gift— His Son! Prayer is as boundless and unlimited as His own blessed Son. There is nothing on earth or in heaven that God's Son did not secure for us. By prayer God gives us the vast and matchless inheritance that is ours by virtue of His Son. God commands us to "come boldly to the throne of grace" (Heb. 4:16). God is glorified and Christ is honored when His children petition Him with big and bold prayers.

Reflection

For which person, circumstance, or need might you boldly pray for today? What kinds of excuses or false views of God may be hindering you from approaching Him with big and bold prayers?

How Strong Is Your Spiritual Desire?

"Blessed are those who hunger and thirst for righteousness, for they shall be filled."

MATTHEW 5:6

We ought to pray whether or not we feel like it and not allow our feelings to determine our habits of prayer. In such circumstance, we ought to pray for the *desire* to pray because such a desire is God-given and heaven-born. Then when desire has been given, we should pray according to its dictates. Lack of spiritual desire should grieve us and lead us to lament its absence, to seek earnestly for its bestowal, so that our praying should be an expression of "the soul's sincere desire."

A sense of need creates—or should create—earnest desire. The stronger the sense of need, the greater should be the desire and the more earnest the praying. Hunger is an active sense of physical need. It prompts the request for bread. In like manner, the inward consciousness of spiritual need creates desire, and desire breaks forth in prayer. Desire is an inward longing for something of which we lack, of which we stand in need—something that God has promised and that may be secured by an earnest supplication of His throne of grace.

Spiritual desire, carried to a higher degree, is the evidence of the new birth. It is born in the renewed soul: "As newborn babes, desire the pure milk of the word, that you may grow thereby" (1 Peter 2:2). The absence of this holy desire in the heart is presumptive proof either of a decline in spiritual zeal or that the new birth has never taken place.

Reflection

What are some of the spiritual danger signs concerning prayer and overall spiritual desire? How strong is your sense of need for God and His blessings?

Heaven: The Horizon of Hope

*"We know that all things work together for good to those who love
God, to those who are the called according to His purpose."*

ROMANS 8:28

The prodigal son was independent and self-sufficient when
in prosperity, but when money and friends vanished and
he began to be in want, he "came to himself" and decided to
return to his father's house, with prayer and confession on his
lips (see Luke 15:11–32). Many a man who has forgotten God
has been stopped, forced to consider his ways, and compelled
to return to the Father. Blessed is trouble when it accomplishes
this in men!

Trouble makes earth undesirable and causes heaven to
loom up large on the horizon of hope. There is a world where
trouble never comes. But the path of tribulation leads to that
world. Those who are there went there through tribulation.
What a world is set before our longing eyes that appeals to our
hopes, as sorrows like a cyclone sweep over us! Hear John, as
he talks about it and those who are there: "I looked, and
behold, a great multitude which no one could number ... [was]
standing before the throne and before the Lamb, clothed with
white robes, with palm branches in their hands.... 'These are
the ones who come out of the great tribulation, and washed
their robes and made them white in the blood of the Lamb'"
(Rev. 7:9, 14).

Oh, children of God, you who have suffered, who have been sorely tried, who bear broken spirits and bleeding hearts, hold fast to the hope on the horizon. God is in all your troubles, and He will see that all will "work together for good" if you will but be patient, submissive, and persevering.

Reflection

Ponder the ways in which your troubles have shaped you. How does looking ahead to heaven sustain you through hardships here on earth?

Two Things God Loathes

"The love of many will grow cold."
MATTHEW 24:12

A lack of passion in prayer is the sure sign of a lack of depth and lack of intensity of desire—and the absence of intense desire is a sure sign of God's absence from the heart! To lose fervor is to retire from God. He can, and does, tolerate many things in the way of infirmity and failings in His children. He can, and will, pardon sin when the penitent person prays. But two things are intolerable to Him—insincerity and luke-warmness. Simply put, lack of heart and lack of heat are two things He loathes.

Reflection

Why does God hate insincerity and lack of spiritual passion and commitment? If you are lacking heart or heat, what can you do to regain them?

Beware of Satan's Craftiness

"Be sober, be vigilant; because your adversary the devil walks about like a roaring lion, seeking whom he may devour."

1 PETER 5:8

Satan perverts the things that are truly works of God and misemploys miracles to obscure God's glory. The Devil often tries to break down the soul and reduce it to despair. He tries to discourage us by telling us we will never succeed. The way is too hard and narrow, and the burden is too heavy.

He takes advantage of faltering faith and foments fears. Grace is hidden from sight, shortcomings are magnified, and infirmities are classed as gross sins. Sometimes Satan uses the fear of death to quench the fire of faith, and the grave becomes something to dread. He darkens the future. Heaven and God will be out of sight, hidden by a thick veil of tomorrow's cares, trials, and needs. The imaginary disasters, failures, and evils of tomorrow are powerful weapons in Satan's hands. He suggests that the Lord is a hard master and that His promises will fail. He works on the remaining corruption in the heart and raises a great storm in the soul. He tempts to evil tempers, to hasty words, to impatience, and to carnal reasoning, which is his powerful ally in our minds.

Reflection

How has Satan tried to deceive you and undermine your faith? Why is the mind such a spiritual battleground?

The Value of Vigilance

"Continue earnestly in prayer, being vigilant in it with thanksgiving."
COLOSSIANS 4:2

Nothing distinguishes the children of God so clearly and strongly as consistent, vigilant prayer. It is the one infallible mark and test of being a Christian. Christian people are prayerful. Worldly minded people are prayerless. Christians call on God. Worldly minded people ignore God and don't call on His name. But even the Christian needs to cultivate continual prayer. Prayer must be habitual, but much more than a habit. It is duty, yet one that rises far above and goes beyond ordinary implications of the term. It is the expression of a relation to God, a yearning for divine communion. It is the outward and upward flow of the inward life toward its original fountain.

Prayer has everything to do with molding the soul into the image of God, with enhancing and enlarging the measure of divine grace, with bringing the soul into complete communion with God, and with enriching the soul's experience of God. Prayer is the only way in which the soul of man can enter into fellowship and communion with God, the source of all Christlike spirit and energy.

Reflection

How can you cultivate "consistent, vigilant prayer"? What challenges do you face in doing this?

Keep Resurrection Truth Prominent

*"Blessed be the God and Father of our Lord Jesus Christ,
who according to His abundant mercy has begotten us again to
a living hope through the resurrection of Jesus Christ from the dead."*

1 PETER 1:3

What a place the resurrection of the dead had in apostolic preaching. Christ was raised from the dead, and those who claim His saving grace will be resurrected with Him. What comfort and solace this message brought to early believers. How often it was repeated to edify, refresh, and strengthen. What a rich message it was for the early church to bear and receive. How well assured the early Christians were of its truth. It belonged to the heart of their faith. It burnished their hopes with a double radiance. It enabled them to endure martyr fires and fierce persecutions.

We need to have these fundamental facts put into our spiritual being anew, like iron put into the blood to make it red, strong, and life-giving. These mighty assurances have, for many believers, lost their energy and their emboldening power. Our faith demands to be fed anew by them.

These facts must be to us what they were to the early Christians—hope, power, and confidence. They must weave our songs and fill our testimony. We must know that Jesus

Christ has been raised from the dead, for we have been raised from the death of sin with Him.

Reflection

Why must we always keep the resurrection of Jesus in mind? What difference should that historical event make in our daily lives?

Warm-Hearted Servants, Red-Hot Prayers

"My soul breaks with longing for Your judgments at all times."
PSALM 119:20

Prayer without fervor stakes nothing on the issue because it has nothing to stake. It comes with empty, listless hands that have never learned the lesson of clinging to the cross. Lethargic prayer has no heart in it; it is a barren thing, an unfit vessel. Heart, soul, and life must find place in all real praying. Heaven must be made to feel the force of this crying out to God.

Paul was a notable example of the man who possessed a fervent spirit of prayer. His petitioning was all consuming, centered immovably on the object of his desire and the God who was able to meet it. Prayers must be red hot. The fervent prayer is effectual and avails. Coldness of spirit hinders praying; prayer cannot live in a wintry atmosphere. Chilly surroundings freeze out petitioning and dry up the springs of supplication. It takes fire to make prayers go. Warmth of soul creates an atmosphere favorable to prayer because it is favorable to fervency. By flame prayer ascends to heaven. Yet fire is not fuss, heat, or noise. Heat is intensity—something that glows and burns. Heaven is a mighty poor market for ice.

God wants warm-hearted servants. The Holy Spirit comes *as a fire* to dwell in us; we are to be baptized with the Holy

Spirit and with fire. Fervency is warmth of soul. A phlegmatic temperament is abhorrent to vital experience. If our religion does not set us on fire, it is because we have frozen hearts. God dwells in a flame; the Holy Spirit descends in fire. To be absorbed in God's will, to be so greatly in earnest about doing it that our whole being takes fire, is the qualifying condition of the person who would engage in effectual prayer.

Reflection

How do our hearts become "frozen"? How can we rekindle our intensity for God and His will? What does it mean to be "absorbed in God's will"?

Zealously Seek the Spirit

"The grace of the Lord Jesus Christ, and the love of God, and the communion of the Holy Spirit be with you all."

2 CORINTHIANS 13:14

Believers want to be filled with the Holy Spirit's power and presence, yet many complain of experiencing a distinct lack of either. Why is this? For so many of God's children, it may truly be said, "You do not have Him because you do not ask." And of many others it might be said, "You have Him in little measure because you pray for Him in little measure." The Holy Spirit is the Spirit of purity, power, holiness, faith, love, and joy. All grace is brought into being and perfected by Him.

We need the Holy Spirit, and we need to stir ourselves up to seek Him. The measure we receive of Him will be gauged by the fervor of faith and prayer with which we seek Him. Our ability to work for God, pray to God, live for God, and affect others for God will be dependent on the measure of the Holy Spirit received by us, dwelling in us, and working through us.

Reflection

Why is our ability to do God's work effectively dependent on receiving the Holy Spirit? How deeply do you desire the Holy Spirit's presence and work in your life?

Earnest Entreaties

"Which of you shall have a friend, and go to him at midnight and say to him, 'Friend, lend me three loaves.' ... I say to you, though he will not rise and give to him because he is his friend, yet because of his persistence he will rise and give him as many as he needs."

LUKE 11:5, 8

The tenor of Christ's teachings is to declare that people are to pray earnestly—to pray with an earnestness that cannot be denied. Heaven has listening ears only for the whole-hearted and the deeply earnest. Energy, courage, and persistent perseverance must back the prayers that heaven respects and God hears.

All these qualities of soul, so essential to effectual praying, are brought out in the parable of the man who, at midnight, went to his friend for bread. This man entered on his errand with confidence. Friendship promised him success. His plea was pressing: Truly he could not go back empty-handed. The flat refusal chagrined and surprised him. Here even friendship failed! But there was something to be tried yet—stern resolution, set and fixed determination. He would stay and press his demand until the door was opened and the request was granted. This he proceeded to do and, by force of importunity, secured what ordinary solicitation had failed to obtain.

The Savior used the success of this man, achieved in the face of a flat denial, to illustrate the necessity for insistence in supplicating the throne of heavenly grace. When the answer is not immediately given, the praying Christian must gather courage at each delay and advance in urgency until the answer comes that is assured if he has but the faith to press his petition with vigorous faith.

Faint-heartedness, impatience, and timidity will be fatal to our prayers. Awaiting the onset of our importunity and insistence is the Father's heart, hand, infinite power, along with His infinite willingness to hear and answer. Persistent praying is the earnest, inward movement of the heart toward God. It is the throwing of the entire force of the spiritual man into the exercise of prayer.

Reflection

Are you constantly bringing your needs before God? Why or why not? What hinders you from making earnest, persistent entreaties to the Lord?

Character Counts

"If indeed you have heard [Christ] and have been taught by Him ...
put on the new man which was created according to God,
in true righteousness and holiness."

EPHESIANS 4:21, 24

Prayer governs conduct, and conduct makes character. Conduct is what we do; character is what we are. Conduct is the outward life. Character is the life unseen, hidden within, yet evidenced by that which *is* seen. Conduct is external, seen from without; character is internal—operating within. In the economy of grace, conduct is the offspring of character. Character is the state of the heart; conduct its outward expression. Character is the root of the tree; conduct is the fruit it bears.

Prayer helps to establish character and fashion conduct, and both depend on prayer for their successful continuance. There may be a certain degree of moral character and conduct independent of prayer, but there cannot be anything like distinctive religious character and Christian conduct without it. Prayer helps where all other aids fail. The more we pray, the better we are, the purer and better our lives become.

The very end and purpose of Christ's atoning work is to create religious character and to make Christian conduct: "Jesus Christ ... gave Himself for us, that He might redeem us from every lawless deed and purify for Himself His own special people, zealous for good works" (Titus 2:13–14).

In Christ's teaching, it is not simply works of charity and deeds of mercy on which He insists, but inward spiritual character. This much is demanded; nothing short of it will suffice. In the study of Paul's Epistles, one thing stands out clearly and unmistakably—the insistence on holiness of heart and righteousness of life.

Reflection

What role does prayer play in helping each of us to be holy and righteous? Does your inward character match your outward conduct?

Distaste for Deceitfulness

*"Bow down Your ear, O LORD, hear me; for I am poor
and needy. Preserve my life, for I am holy; You are my God;
save your servant who trusts in You!"*

PSALM 86:1–2

Prayer produces cleanliness of heart and purity of life. It can produce nothing else. Unrighteous conduct is born of prayerlessness; the two go hand in hand. Prayer and sinning cannot keep company with each other. One or the other must, of necessity, stop.

Get men to pray, and they will quit sinning because prayer creates distaste for deceitfulness and so works on the heart that evildoing becomes repugnant and the entire nature is lifted to a reverent contemplation of high and holy things.

Reflection

How has prayer influenced your attitudes and actions? Which areas of sin still may be keeping you from holiness?

A Remedy for Temptation

"When Jesus perceived that [the people] were about to come and take Him by force to make Him king, He departed again to the mountain by Himself alone."

JOHN 6:15

The multitudes had been fed and were dismissed by our Lord. Then, knowing they wanted to make Him their earthly ruler, He went away from the eager, anxious, seeking multitudes. The mass of needy people taxed and exhausted Him; the disciples were tossed on the sea, but calmness reigned on the mountaintop where our Lord was kneeling in secret prayer. He needed to be alone in that moment with God. Temptation was in that hour.

The multitude had feasted on the five loaves and the two fishes. Filled with food and excited beyond measure, they would make Him king. He fled from the temptation to secret prayer, for here was the source of His strength to resist evil. What a refuge was secret prayer, even to Him! What a refuge it is to us from the world's dazzling and delusive crowns. What safety there is to be alone with God when the world tempts us, allures us, and attracts us.

Reflection

Generally, how do you respond when temptations come? Do you seek God's presence and power … and pray?

False Standards of Church Strength

"Christ also loved the church and gave Himself for her, that He might sanctify and cleanse her with the washing of water by the word ... that she should be holy and without blemish."

EPHESIANS 5:25–27

One of Satan's schemes to debase and deceive is to establish a wrong estimate of church strength. He marshals and parades the most engaging material results, lauds the power of civilizing forces, and makes the church's glories and power be proclaimed until church leaders are dazzled and ensnared. The church becomes thoroughly worldly while boasting of her spirituality.

No deceiver is so artful in the diabolical trade of deception as Satan. As an angel of light, he leads a soul to death. To mistake the elements of church strength is to mistake the character of the church and also to change its character—all its efforts and aims. The strength of the church lies in its piety, purity, and humility. All else is incidental and is not of the strength of things. But in worldly, popular language of this day, a church is called strong when its membership is large, when it has social position and financial resources, when ability and eloquence fill the pulpit, and when the pews are filled by polished, prestigious people. Bear in mind the truth: Church strength does not consist in its numbers and its money, but in the holiness of its members.

Reflection

What happens when the church allows earthly values to be its standard rather than the standards of God? Think about some ways in which false standards may be influencing your local church and how you might address this issue.

Obedience Is Not Optional

"If you keep My commandments, you will abide in My love, just as I have kept My Father's commandments and abide in His love."

JOHN 15:10

What a marvelous statement of the relationship created and maintained by obedience! The Son of God is held in the bosom of the Father's love by virtue of His obedience. And the factor that enables the Son of God to abide always in His Father's love is revealed in His own statement, "I always do those things that please Him" (John 8:29).

The gift of the Holy Spirit in full measure and in richer experience depends on loving obedience: "If you love Me, keep My commandments. And I will pray the Father, and He will give you another Helper, that He may abide with you forever" (John 14:15–16). Obedience to God is a condition of spiritual thrift, inward satisfaction, and stability of heart. "If you are willing and obedient, you shall eat the good of the land" (Isa. 1:19). Obedience opens the gates of the Holy City and gives access to the tree of life. "Blessed are those who do His commandments, that they may have the right to the tree of life, and may enter through the gates into the city" (Rev. 22:14).

What is obedience? It is doing God's will; it is keeping His commandments. Does God give commandments that people cannot obey? Is He so arbitrary, severe, and unloving as to issue commandments that can't be obeyed? The answer is that in all the annals of Holy Scripture, not a single instance is recorded of God having commanded any man to do a thing that was beyond his power. Is God so unjust and inconsiderate as to require of man that which he is unable to render? Surely not. To infer it is to slander God's character.

Reflection

Why does God command each of us to obey Him, no matter how difficult that may be sometimes? In which areas do you have the most difficult time obeying God? To what extent are you experiencing the Holy Spirit's enabling power in dealing with difficulties in obeying God?

The Demands of Prayer

"I beg you, brethren, through the Lord Jesus Christ, and through the love of the Spirit, that you strive together with me in prayers to God for me, that I may be delivered from those in Judea who do not believe."

ROMANS 15:30–31

Paul had foes in Judea—foes who beset and opposed him. And this, added to other weighty reasons, led him to urge the Roman Christians to "strive together" with him in prayers. That word *strive* indicated wrestling, the putting forth of great effort. This is the kind of effort, and this the sort of spirit, that must possess the Christian soldier.

Here is a great soldier, a captain-general, in the great struggle, faced by malignant forces who seek his ruin. His force is nearly spent. What reinforcements can he count on? What can give help and bring success to a warrior during such a pressing emergency? It is a critical moment in the conflict. What force can be added to the energy of his own prayers? The answer is—the prayers of others.

The Christian soldier is to pray at all times and under all circumstances. His praying must be arranged in order to cover his times of peace as well as his hours of active conflict. It must be available during his marching and his fighting. Prayer must diffuse all effort, saturate all ventures, and decide all issues. The Christian soldier must be as intense in his praying as in his fighting, because his victories will depend very much more on his praying than on his fighting. Fervent supplication must be added to steady resolve; prayer and supplication must supplement the armor of God. The Holy Spirit must aid the supplication with His own strenuous plea, and the soldier must pray in the Spirit. In this, as in other forms of warfare, eternal vigilance is the price of victory. Thus watchfulness and persistent perseverance must mark every activity of the Christian warrior.

Reflection

In your daily life, what types of spiritual battles do you face? How are you responding to them? What role does prayer have in your warfare-related activities?

Fully Test God's Promises

---

*"May the LORD God of your fathers ...
bless you as He has promised you!"*

DEUTERONOMY 1:11

We should humbly receive the utmost reach and full benefit of the rich promises of the Word of God and put them to the test. The world will never receive the full benefits of the gospel until this is done. Neither Christian experiences nor Christian living will be what they ought to be until those who pray fully test these divine promises. By prayer, we bring these promises of God's holy will into the realm of the actual and the real. Prayer is the philosopher's stone that transmutes them into gold.

If someone asks what is to be done in order to render God's promises real, the answer is that we must pray until the words of the promise are clothed with the rich raiment of fulfillment.

Reflection

How does your view of God—who He is, how He responds—influence your willingness to test His promises in the Bible? What's the difference between believing God's promises and trying to "name it and claim it"?

What Matters Most with God

"Hear the word of the LORD, you rulers of Sodom; give ear to the law of our God, you people of Gomorrah.... Even though you make many prayers, I will not hear. Your hands are full of blood."

ISAIAH 1:10, 15

With God, character and integrity matter most. He sees the heart of man, and this is of most significance and consequence. What we are with God gauges our influence with Him. It was the inner character, not the outward appearance, of such men as Abraham, Job, David, Moses, and all others that had such great influence with God in the days of old. And today, it is not so much our words but what we really are that counts with God. Conduct affects character, of course, and counts for much in our praying. At the same time, character affects conduct to a far greater extent and has a superior influence over praying. Our inner life not only gives color to our praying, but body as well.

Bad living means bad praying and, in the end, no praying at all. We pray feebly because we live feebly. The stream of prayer cannot rise higher than the fountain of living. The force of the inner chamber is made up of the energy that flows from the confluent streams of living. And the weakness of living grows out of shallowness and shoddiness of character.

Feebleness of living reflects its debility and languor in the praying hours. We simply cannot talk to God, strongly and intimately and confidently, unless we are living for Him faithfully and truly. The prayer closet cannot become sanctified to God when the life is alien to His precepts and purpose. We must learn this lesson well. Righteous character and Christlike conduct give us a peculiar and preferential standing in prayer before God.

Reflection

Are you faithfully and truly living for God? In which areas might you be disobeying God and His laws? What do you think the author meant by the term "feebleness of living"?

Faith in Christ, Fruitfulness in Prayer

"Most assuredly, I say to you, he who believes in Me, the works that I do he will do also.... And whatever you ask in My name, that I will do, that the Father may be glorified in the Son."

JOHN 14:12–13

Faith in Christ is the basis of all working and all praying. All wonderful works depend on wonderful praying, and all praying is done in the name of Jesus Christ. An amazing lesson, of wondrous simplicity, is this praying in the name of the Lord Jesus! All other conditions are depreciated, everything else is renounced, except Jesus. The name of Jesus must be supremely sovereign during the hour of prayer.

If Jesus dwells at the fountain of my life, if obedience to Him is the inspiration and force of every movement of my life, then He can pledge Himself, by an obligation as profound as His own nature, that whatsoever is asked will be granted. Nothing can be clearer, more distinct, and more unlimited both in application and extent than the exhortation and urgency of Christ: "Have faith in God."

Reflection

Why is effective prayer dependent upon faith in Christ? Why is it important to keep prayer centered on Jesus' power and authority?

How Deeply Do You Desire God?

*"Because you are lukewarm, and neither cold nor hot,
I will vomit you out of My mouth."*

REVELATION 3:16

Do we feel a profound sense of longing for communion with God? Do we feel the inward pantings of desire after heavenly treasures? Do deep desires stir our souls to seek after Him? Oh, how frequently the fire of our heart burns altogether too low. The flaming heat of soul has been tempered down to a tepid lukewarmness. This, it should be remembered, was the central cause of the sad and desperate condition of the Laodicean Christians, of whom the awful condemnation is written that they were "rich," had "become wealthy," and had "need of nothing" and didn't know that they were "wretched, miserable, poor, blind, and naked" (Rev. 3:17).

Have we that desire that presses us to close communion with God, which is filled with unutterable burnings and holds us there through the agony of an intense and soul-stirred supplication? Our hearts need much to be worked over, not only to get the evil out of them but to get the good into them. And the foundation of and inspiration for the incoming good is strong, propelling desire. This holy and fervid flame in the soul awakens heaven's interest, attracts God's attention, and places at the disposal of those who exercise it the exhaustless riches of divine grace.

Reflection

How can believers recognize that they are "lukewarm"? What are some internal and external signs of this?

The Church: A House of Prayer

"My house shall be called a house of prayer."
MATTHEW 21:13

Prayer should always be a central feature in the house of God. When prayer is a stranger there, it ceases to be God's house. Our Lord put peculiar emphasis on what the church was when He cast out the buyers and sellers in the temple, repeating these words from Isaiah: "It is written, 'My house shall be called a house of prayer'" (Matt. 21:13). He makes prayer preeminent, that which stands out above all else in the house of God. People who minimize prayer and give it a secondary place undermine the church of God and make it something less than it is ordained to be.

The church's life, power, and glory is prayer. The life of its members is dependent on prayer, and God's presence is secured and retained by prayer. The very place is made sacred by its ministry. Without it, the church is lifeless and powerless. Without it, even the building itself is nothing, more or other, than any other structure. Prayer converts even the bricks, mortar, and lumber, into a sanctuary, a holy of holies where the presence of God dwells. Without prayer, the building may be costly, perfect in all its appointments, beautiful for situation, and attractive to the eye, but it comes down to the human, with nothing divine in it, and is on a level with all other buildings.

Reflection

Why do you think so many churches today devote relatively little time to prayer? What might believers do to encourage more prayer in their churches?

Matters of the Heart

*"The gospel which was preached by me is not according to man.
For I neither received it from man, nor was I taught it,
but it came through the revelation of Jesus Christ."*

GALATIANS 1:11–12

Great men and great minds are neither the channels nor depositories of God's revelation by virtue of their culture, intellect, or wisdom. God's system in redemption and providence is not to be thought out, open only to the learned and wise. The learned and the wise, following their learning and their wisdom, have always sadly and darkly missed God's thoughts and God's ways.

The condition of receiving God's revelation and of holding God's truth is one of the heart, not one of the head. The ability to receive and search out is like that of the child, full of innocence and simplicity. These are the conditions on which God reveals Himself to men. The world by wisdom cannot know God. The world by wisdom can never receive or understand God because God reveals Himself to men's hearts, not to their heads. Only hearts can ever know God, feel God, see God, and read God in His Book of Books. God is not grasped by thought but by feeling. The world gets God by revelation, not by philosophy. It is not apprehension—the mental ability to grasp God—but plasticity, ability to be impressed, that men need. It is not by hard, strong, stern, great reasoning that the world gets God or gets hold of God, but by big, soft, pure hearts. Men need hearts to feel God much more than they need light to see God.

Reflection

Why can't people know God through their earthly wisdom? What happens when people build foundations for spiritual faith on their intellect rather than the heart? In what ways has God revealed Himself to you?

Time Alone with God

---

*"And when He had sent the multitudes away, [Jesus] went up
on the mountain by Himself to pray."*

MATTHEW 14:23

Jesus Christ was the preeminent teacher of prayer by precept
and example. His instruction on the nature and necessity of
prayer, as recorded in the gospels, is remarkable. We see how
the whole of Jesus' life was saturated with continual conversation and communion with the Father. Although He did not
hesitate to utter prayers in the presence of other people, we
can't help but notice how often He went away by Himself for
solitary prayer. Likewise, He told His followers to retreat to
their prayer closets, to avoid the temptation of public display
and, presumably, the distractions that so easily divert the mind
from God.

Prayer must be a holy exercise, untainted by vanity or
pride. It must be in secret. God lives there, is sought there, and
is found there.

Reflection

Why is time alone with God so important? How might you
allot more time and space for solitary prayer?

God, Our Father

"Our Father in heaven, hallowed be Your name."
LUKE 11:2

The Jewish law and the prophets knew something of God as a Father. They had occasional and imperfect, yet comforting, glimpses of the great truth of God's Fatherhood and of our relationship to Him as children. Christ laid the foundation of prayer deep and strong with this basic principle. The law of prayer, the right to pray, rests on the Father-child relationship. "Our Father" brings us into the closest connection with God.

Prayer is the child's approach, the child's plea, and the child's right. It is the law of prayer that looks up, that lifts up the eye to "Our Father in heaven." Our Father's house is our home in heaven. Heavenly citizenship and heavenly homesickness are found in prayer. Prayer is an appeal from the lowness, from the emptiness, and from the need of earth to the highness, the fullness, and the all-sufficiency of heaven. Prayer turns the eye and the heart heavenward with a child's longing, a child's trust, and a child's expectancy.

Reflection

Think about how you might approach God—your heavenly Father—with a child's longings, trust, and expectancy. If you don't already do so, how might you pray like this every day?

God's Promises: Receive and Believe

"You shall call, and the LORD will answer;
you shall cry, and He will say, 'Here I am.'"

ISAIAH 58:9

God's promises lie like giant corpses without life, only for decay and dust, unless men appropriate and give life to these promises by earnest and prevailing prayer. The answer to prayer is assured not only by the promises of God, but also by God's relation to us as a Father: "But you, when you pray, go into your room, and when you have shut your door, pray to your Father who is in the secret place; and your Father who sees in secret will reward you openly" (Matt. 6:6).

God encourages us to pray, not only because of the certainty of the answer but because of the generosity of the promise and the bounty of the giver. The challenge of God to us is, "Call to Me, and I will answer you, and show you great and mighty things, which you do not know" (Jer. 33:3).

Reflection

Why do you think God is so eager for you to call out to Him? How can you "activate" His promises in your life?

Unforgiveness Hinders Prayer

*"Therefore if you bring your gift to the altar, and there remember
that your brother has something against you, leave your gift there
before the altar, and go your way. First be reconciled to your
brother, and then come and offer your gift."*

MATTHEW 5:23–24

He who tries to pray to God with an angry spirit, with an
unreconciled heart, and with unsettled neighborly scores
spends his labor for that which is worse than nothing. For
grudges, bitterness, and acrimony violate the law of prayer.

Indeed, how rigidly exacting is Christ's law of prayer! It
goes to the heart and demands that love be enthroned there—
love for the brotherhood. The sacrifice of prayer must be
seasoned and perfumed with love—love fully dwelling in heart,
mind, and soul.

Reflection

Why must praying people hold no grudges? Is there someone you need to seek forgiveness from—or offer forgiveness to?

Seek God's Power for Tasks

"Teacher, I brought You my son, who has a mute spirit. And whenever it seizes him, it throws him down; he foams at the mouth, gnashes his teeth, and becomes rigid. So I spoke to Your disciples, that they should cast it out, but they could not."

MARK 9:17–18

As Jesus came down from the Mount of Transfiguration, He found His disciples defeated, humiliated, and confused in the presence of their enemies. A father had brought his demon-possessed child to have the demon cast out. They tried to do it but failed. They had been commissioned by Jesus and sent to do that very work, but their efforts were futile. "And when he had come into the house, His disciples asked Him privately, 'Why could we not cast it out?' So He said to them, 'This kind can come out by nothing but by prayer and fasting'" (Mark 9:28–29).

The disciples' faith had not been cultured by prayer. They failed in prayer before they failed in ability to do their work. They failed in faith because they had failed in prayer. The one thing that was necessary to do God's work was prayer. The work that God sends us to do cannot be done without prayer.

Reflection

Do you pray regularly about your activities, about the daily work that God has called you to do? What kinds of things keep you from praying about everything—including your day-to-day responsibilities?

Ask, Seek, and Knock

"Ask, and it will be given to you; seek, and you will find;
knock, and it will be opened to you."

MATTHEW 7:7

O ur Lord laid Himself out to make it clear and strong that
God answers prayer—assuredly, certainly, inevitably. Jesus
said that it is the duty of the child to ask and to persevere—and
that the Father is obliged to answer and to give for the asking.

In Christ's teaching, prayer is not a sterile, vain performance. It is not a mere rite or ritual but a request for an answer,
a plea to gain, the seeking of a great good from God. It is a lesson of getting that for which we ask, of finding that for which
we seek, and of entering the door at which we knock.

Reflection

How might the prayers of some believers change if they
viewed prayer in this light? Why does prayer sometimes
become a ritual rather than a dynamic interaction with God?

A Defense against Evil

"He shall call upon Me, and I will answer him; I will be with him in trouble; I will deliver him and honor him."

PSALM 91:15

During the last of His earthly life, Christ urged prayer as a preventive and precautionary tool against the many evils to which His disciples were exposed. In view of the temporal and fearful terrors of the destruction of Jerusalem, He charges them to this effect: "Pray that your flight may not be in winter" (Matt. 24:20).

How many evils in this life can be escaped by prayer. How many fearful, temporal calamities can be mitigated, if not wholly relieved, by prayer. Notice how, amid the excesses and overwhelming influences to which we are exposed in this world, Christ charges us to pray: "Take heed to yourselves, lest … that Day come on you unexpectedly. For it will come as a snare on all those who dwell on the face of the whole earth. Watch therefore, and pray always that you may be counted worthy to escape all these things … and to stand before the Son of Man" (Luke 21:34–36).

Reflection

In which areas are you exposed to evil influences? How might prayer make a positive difference in facing these influences?

Bathe Your Work in Prayer

*"[Jesus] went out to the mountain to pray,
and continued all night in prayer to God."*

LUKE 6:12

Jesus was always a busy man with His work, but He was never too busy to pray. The most divine of business filled His heart and filled His hands, consumed His time, and exhausted His nerves. But with Him even God's work did not crowd out God's praying. Saving people from sin or suffering must not be substituted for praying, nor reduce in the least the time or intensity of this holiest of activities. Jesus filled the day with working for God; He used the night to pray to God. The day-working made the night-praying a necessity. The night-praying sanctified and made successful the day-working.

Reflection

How does the truth of this reading apply to you—your work, daily activities, goals, and dreams? How can you allocate more time to bathe your work in prayer?

God's Word: A Sure Foundation

"Your word is a lamp to my feet and a light to my path."

PSALM 119:105

Faith accepts the Bible as the Word and will of God and rests upon its truth without question and without other evidence. Faith accepts the Word of God as unquestionable evidence of any fact and rejoices in the fact as true because God asserts it in His Word.

Many of the facts revealed to us in the Bible receive the credence of our reason as fit and proper things. Other facts extend beyond the range of reason, and it has neither vision nor analogy to measure them. Whether God's Word *confirms* the beliefs we already have or *challenges* the ones we're wrestling with, we can be assured that every principle and precept revealed is absolutely true.

Reflection

What happens when people "pick and choose" which truths of the Bible to obey? How does the Bible serve as a foundation for those who believe in its absolute truth?

Wonderful Praying, Wonderful Results

*"If you then, being evil, know how to give good gifts to your children,
how much more will your Father who is in heaven
give good things to those who ask Him!"*

MATTHEW 7:11

With Moses, the great features of prayer were prominent. He never beat the air or fought a sham battle. The most serious and strenuous business of his serious and strenuous life was prayer. He was at it with the most intense earnestness of his soul. Intimate as he was with God, his intimacy did not abate the necessity of prayer. This intimacy only brought clearer insight into the nature and necessity of prayer, and led him to see the greater obligations to pray and discover the larger results of praying.

In reviewing one crisis through which Israel passed, he wrote, "I prostrated myself before the LORD; forty days and forty nights I kept prostrating myself" (Deut. 9:25). Wonderful praying and wonderful results! Moses knew how to engage in wonderful praying, and God knew how to give wonderful results.

The whole force of biblical statement is to increase our faith in the doctrine that prayer affects God and secures favors from God that can be secured in no other way and that God won't bestow if we don't pray. The whole canon of Bible teaching illustrates the great truth that God hears and answers prayer. One of God's great purposes in His Word is to impress on us indelibly the great importance, priceless value, and absolute necessity of asking Him for things we need for time and eternity. He urges us by every consideration, and presses and warns us by every interest. He points us to His Son, turned over to us for our good, as His pledge that prayer will be answered, teaching us that God is our Father, able to do all things for us and give all things to us, much more than earthly parents are able or willing to do for their children.

Reflection

How might your life be different if you, like Moses, dedicated more time to the serious business of praying? What makes prayer "strenuous" rather than easy?

Combating Satan

"In his upper room, with his windows open toward Jerusalem, [Daniel] knelt down on his knees three times that day, and prayed and gave thanks before his God, as was his custom since early days."

DANIEL 6:10

Our one great business is prayer, and we will never do it well unless we fasten to it with all binding force. We will never do it well without arranging the best conditions of doing it well. Satan has suffered so much by good praying that he will use all his wily, shrewd, and ensnaring devices to cripple its performances.

We must, by all the fastenings we can find, cable ourselves to prayer. To be loose in time and place is to open the door to Satan. To be exact, prompt, unswerving, and careful in even the little things is to buttress ourselves against the evil one.

Reflection

What kinds of "devices" does Satan use to cripple our praying? Which ones has he used to try to cripple *your* praying?

Little with God, Little for God

*"It is good for me to draw near to God;
I have put my trust in the Lord GOD."*

PSALM 73:28

O ur devotions are not measured by the clock, but time is of their essence. Short devotions are the bane of deep piety. Calmness, grasp, and strength are never the companions of hurry. Short devotions deplete spiritual vigor, arrest spiritual progress, sap spiritual foundations, and blight the root and bloom of spiritual life. They are the prolific source of backsliding, the sure indication of a superficial piety. They deceive, blight, rot the seed, and impoverish the soil.

Spiritual work is taxing work, and men are reluctant to do it. Meeting with God and deeply studying His Word requires an outlay of serious attention and time, which flesh and blood do not relish. Few people are made of such strong fiber that they will make a costly outlay when superficial effort will suffice in other aspects of life. We can habituate ourselves to our meager effort until it looks good to us; at least it keeps up a decent form and quiets conscience—the deadliest of opiates. We can curtail our time with God and not realize the peril until the foundations are gone. Hurried devotions make weak faith, feeble convictions, and questionable piety. To be little *with* God is to be little *for* God.

Reflection

Why do so many people avoid unhurried and longer time with God? What can you expect to happen when you don't make the effort to spend deep, enriching time with God?

Pray Expectantly

"Ask, and you will receive, that your joy may be full."
JOHN 16:24

We have much fine writing and learned talk about the subjective benefits of prayer—how prayer secures its full measure of results, not by affecting God but by affecting us. We are taught by such teachers that the province of prayer is not to *receive* from God, but to *train* us to be godly. Prayer thus becomes a mere performance, a drill sergeant, a school in which patience, tranquility, and dependence are taught. In this school denial of prayer is the most valuable teacher.

How well all this may look, and how reasonable it may seem, but there is nothing of it in the Bible. The clear and often repeated language of the Bible is that God answers prayer, that He occupies the relation of a heavenly Father to us, and that as Father He gives us the things for which we ask. The best praying, therefore, gets an answer.

Reflection

In what ways have you been influenced by people who have cautioned you not to expect God to answer your prayers? How does such teaching affect people's desire to pray?

The Advantages of Adversity

*"May the God of all grace, who called us to His eternal glory
by Christ Jesus, after you have suffered a while, perfect,
establish, strengthen, and settle you."*

1 PETER 5:10

It is in the fires of suffering that God purifies His saints and brings them to the highest things. It is in the furnace that their faith is tested, their patience is tried, and they are developed in all those rich virtues that make up Christian character. It is while they are passing through deep waters that He shows how close He can come to His praying, believing saints.

It takes faith of a high order and a Christian experience far above the average religion of this day to count it joy when we are called to pass through tribulation. God's highest aim in dealing with His people is to develop Christian character. He is after producing in us those rich virtues that belong to our Lord Jesus Christ. He is seeking to make us like Himself. It is not so much work that He wants in us. It is not greatness. It is the presence in us of patience, meekness, submission to the divine will, and prayerfulness that brings everything to Him. He seeks to beget His own image in us. Trouble in some form tends to do this very thing, for this is the end and aim of trouble. This is its work. This is the task it is called to perform. It is not a chance incident in life, but has a design in view, just as it has an all-wise Designer behind it who makes trouble His agent to bring forth the largest results.

Reflection

How might our perspectives on our suffering change if we really believe the truths in this reading? What might God be trying to accomplish through the trouble in *your* life?

A Child's Cry, A Father's Response

"I will praise You, for You have answered me, and have become my salvation."

PSALM 118:21

Prayer is not a mere habit, riveted by custom and memory, some task to be completed. Prayer is not a duty that must be performed to ease obligation and quiet conscience. Prayer is not mere privilege, a sacred indulgence to be taken advantage of at leisure, at pleasure, at will, with no serious loss attending its omission.

Prayer is a solemn service due to God, an adoration, a worship, the presenting of some desire, the expression of some need to Him, who supplies all need and satisfies all desires, who as a Father finds His greatest pleasure in relieving the wants and granting the desires of His children. Prayer is the child's request, not to the winds or the world, but to the Father. Prayer is the outstretched arms of the child for the Father's help. Prayer is the child's cry calling to the Father's ear, the Father's heart, and the Father's ability, which the Father is to hear, feel, and relieve.

Reflection

Do you view prayer as a "child's cry" to a loving Father? How can you develop a closer relationship with your heavenly Father?

God's Word: Alive in You

"If You abide in Me, and My words abide in you, you will ask what you desire, and it shall be done for you."

Here we have a fixed attitude of life as the condition of prayer. Not simply a fixed attitude of life toward some great principles or purposes, but the fixed attitude and unity of life with Jesus Christ. To live in Him, to be one with Him, to draw all life from Him, to let all life from Him flow through us—this is the attitude of prayer and the ability to pray. No abiding in Him can be separated from His Word abiding in us. It must live in us to give birth to prayer and give food for prayer. The attitude of the person of Christ is the condition of prayer.

The Old Testament saints had been taught that God had magnified His Word above all His name (see Ps. 138:2). New Testament saints must learn fully how to exalt by perfect obedience that Word issuing from the lips of Him who is the Word. Praying people under Christ must learn what praying people under Moses had already learned, that "man shall not live by bread alone, but by every word that proceeds from the mouth of God" (Matt. 4:4). The life of Christ flowing through us and the words of Christ living in us give potency to prayer. They breathe the spirit of prayer and make the body, blood, and bones of prayer. Then it is Christ praying in me and through me.

Reflection

Think about your study of the Bible and your prayer times in light of this reading. What is involved in living according to God's Word? How strong is your commitment to do this?

Expect Repercussions for Following Christ

"I do not pray that You should take them out of the world, but that You should keep them from the evil one. They are not of the world, just as I am not of the world."

JOHN 17:15–16

How the world seduces, dazzles, and deludes the children of God! Christ's disciples are chosen out of the world, out of its bustle and earthliness, out of its all-devouring greed of gain, out of its money desire, money love, and money toil. Earth draws and holds as if it were made out of gold and not out of dirt, as if it were covered with diamonds and not with graves.

"They are not of the world, just as I am not of the world." Not only from sin and Satan were the disciples to be kept, but also from the soil, stain, and taint of worldliness, as Christ was free from it. Their relationship to Christ was not only to free them from the world's defiling taint, its unhallowed love, and its criminal friendships, but the world's hatred would inevitably follow their Christlikeness. No result so necessarily and universally follows its cause as this: "The world has hated them because they are not of the world, just as I am not of the world" (John 17:14).

How pronounced, radical, and eternal was our Lord Christ's divorce from the world! How pronounced, radical, and eternal is that of our Lord's true followers from the world! The world hates the disciple as it hated the Lord and will crucify the disciple just as it crucified his Lord. How pertinent this question is: Have we followed Christ's example of being *in* the world but not *of* the world?

Reflection

Do you suffer the consequences of your Christlikeness, or have you allowed the world to guide your actions and thoughts? What exactly does it mean to be in the world but not of it?

Called to Serious Prayer

*"Be merciful to me, O Lord,
for I cry to You all day long."*

Prayer is no petty invention of man, a fancied relief for fancied ills. Prayer is no dreary performance, dead and death-dealing. Prayer is God's enabling act for man, living and life-giving, joy and joy-giving. Prayer is the contact of a living soul with God. In prayer, God stoops to kiss man, to bless man, and to aid man in everything that God can devise or man can need. Prayer fills man's emptiness with God's fullness, man's poverty with God's riches, man's weakness with God's strength. It banishes man's littleness with God's greatness. Prayer is God's plan to supply man's great and continuous need with His great and continuous abundance.

What is this prayer to which men are called? It is not a mere form, a child's play. It is serious and difficult work, the manliest, mightiest, and most divine work man can do. Prayer lifts men out of the earthly and links them with the heavenly. Men are never nearer heaven and nearer God, never more Godlike, never in deeper sympathy and truer partnership with Jesus Christ than when praying.

Reflection

How is this perspective of prayer different from what you may have heard or learned? Take time now to pray and thank

God for His faithfulness and desire to draw near to you, hear your prayers, and answer your prayers in ways you cannot even imagine.

The Damage of Disunity

*"That they all may be one, as You, Father, are in Me,
and I in You; that they also may be one in Us, that
the world may believe that You sent Me."*

JOHN 17:21

Notice how intently Christ's heart was set on this unity.
What shameful history and what bloody annals has this
lack of unity written for God's church—these walls of separation, alienation, and division that so harm the cause of Christ.
The unity of God's people was to be the heritage of God's glory
promised to them. Contention and conflict are the Devil's
bequest to the church, a heritage of failure, weakness, shame,
and woe.

The oneness of God's people was to be their credential to
the world of the divinity of Christ's mission on earth. Let us ask
in all candor, are we ardently pursuing the kind of unity Christ
prayed for? Are we seeking the peace, welfare, glory, and divinity of God's cause as it is found in the unity of God's people?

Reflection

Where does unity among Christians come from? Are you
praying about unity—among family members, among people
who attend your church, among Christians as a whole? What
might you do to promote unity this coming week?

What the Church Needs

*"My speech and my preaching were not with persuasive words of
human wisdom, but in demonstration of the Spirit and of power, that
your faith should not be in the wisdom of men but in the power of God."*

1 CORINTHIANS 2:4–5

What the church needs today is not better machinery and
operations, not new programs and plans, not more efficient methods and organizations. What the church needs are
people whom the Holy Spirit can use—people fully surrendered to God, people devoted to holiness, people willing to
sacrifice all for the cause of Christ. The Holy Spirit does not
flow through methods, but through people. He does not dwell
in machinery, but in people. He does not anoint plans, but
godly people.

If the church is going to transform this world, it needs
people willing to be transformed into vessels for God's use.

Reflection

What happens when churches emphasize programs
instead of the holiness of its people? How willing are you to be
transformed by God so you can fully participate in His world-
changing mission?

Prayer: Action and Reaction

*"Having been set free from sin ... you have your
fruit to holiness, and the end, everlasting life."*

ROMANS 6:22

Christ constantly and earnestly declared that He came to do His Father's will and not His own will. Likewise, he who follows Christ in prayer must have God's will as his law, rule, and inspiration. The life and the character flow into the prayer closet. There is a mutual action and reaction. The closet has much to do with making the character; the character has much to do with making the closet. "The effective, fervent prayer of a righteous man avails much" (James 5:16).

Christ was the greatest of all praying people because He was the holiest of men. His character is the praying character. His Spirit is the life and power of prayer. A person who has the greatest fluency, the most brilliant imagination, the richest gifts, and the most fiery ardor is not the best prayer, but he who has most imbibed the Spirit of Christ.

Reflection

What does "holiness" involve? How has your character influenced your praying? How has your praying influenced your character?

Heart Conditions

"I will give them a heart to know Me."
JEREMIAH 24:7

The heart, not the head, determines the quality of one's spiritual devotion. It is the heart that surrenders the life to love and fidelity. It is easier to fill the head than it is to prepare the heart. It is easier to make a brain sermon than a heart sermon. It was heart that drew the Son of God from heaven. It is heart that will draw men to heaven. The world needs people with holy, loving hearts to sympathize with its woe, to wipe away its tears, and to alleviate its pain. Christ was eminently the man of sorrows because He was preeminently the man of heart.

"Give me your heart" is God's requisition of His children. He who does not sow with his heart will never reap a harvest for God.

Reflection

Why is there so much emphasis in some Christian circles on the mind rather than the heart? What qualities are exemplified by a holy, loving heart?

Securing God's Fullest Power

"It came to pass that Jesus also was baptized; and while He prayed, the heaven was opened. And the Holy Spirit descended in bodily form like a dove upon Him."

LUKE 3:21–22

The prayers of our Lord illustrated the great truth that the greatest measure of the Holy Spirit, the attesting voice and opening heavens, are only secured by prayer. This is suggested by His baptism by John the Baptist. When Jesus prayed as He was baptized, immediately the Holy Spirit descended on Him like a dove.

More than illustrative was this hour to Him. This critical hour was real and personal, consecrating and qualifying Him for God's highest purposes. Prayer to Him, just as it is to us, was a necessity, an absolute and invariable condition of securing God's fullest, consecrating, and qualifying power. The Holy Spirit came on Him in fullness of measure and power in the very act of prayer. And so the Holy Spirit comes on us, in fullness of measure and power, only in answer to ardent and intense praying.

Reflection

Do you agree that prayer is a necessary condition of receiving God's fullest power? What exactly is "ardent and intense" prayer?

Compelled by Compassion

"We do not have a High Priest who cannot sympathize with our weaknesses, but was in all points tempted as we are, yet without sin."

HEBREWS 4:15

We have a compassionate Savior, one who "can have compassion on those who are ignorant and going astray" (Heb. 5:2). The compassion of our Lord well fits Him for being the Great High Priest of Adam's fallen, lost, and helpless race. And if He is filled with such compassion that it moves Him at the Father's right hand to intercede for us, then we should have the same compassion on the lost.

To the degree in which we are compassionate, we will be prayerful for others. Compassion drives us to our knees in prayer for those who need Christ and His grace. Compassion compels us to be generous and loving that we might point the way to God.

Reflection

How is compassion demonstrated in our day-to-day lives? To whom in your circle of friends and acquaintances can you show love and compassion this week?

118

The God Who Hears

"Jesus lifted up His eyes and said, 'Father, I thank You that You have heard Me.'"

JOHN 11:41

At the grave of Lazarus, as a condition of calling him back to life, our Lord called on His Father in heaven. The lifting to heaven of Christ's eyes—how much there was in it. How much confidence and plea there was in that look toward heaven. His very look, the lifting up of His eyes, carried His whole being heavenward, caused a pause in that world, and drew attention and help. All heaven was engaged, pledged, and moved when the Son of God looked up at this grave.

O for a people with the Christlike eye, heaven lifted and heaven arresting! As it was with Christ, so ought we to be so perfected in faith, so skilled in praying, that we could lift our eyes to heaven and say with Him, with deepest humility and commanding confidence, "Father, I thank You that You have heard me."

Reflection

Do you feel that God hears you when you call to Him for help? In what ways have you looked to heaven for assistance recently?

Jesus Triumphed over Death

"The sting of death is sin.... But thanks be to God, who gives us the victory through our Lord Jesus Christ."

1 CORINTHIANS 15:56–57

In the person of Jesus—His acts and teachings—death holds an essential, conspicuous place. It could not be otherwise. Death holds a commanding and ruinous reign over the race that Jesus Christ came to redeem. There could be no redemption of man without an invasion of the realms of death. There could be no sunlight to humanity while the clouds and night of death hung heavy and dread. The Emancipator had to break the bonds that held, throttled, and enslaved.

Christ came to confront death, to dismantle its empire, to discrown its king until every one of Christ's imprisoned ones will shout, "Death is swallowed up in victory. O Death, where is your sting? O Hades, where is your victory?" (1 Cor. 15:54–55). The resurrection is the rich jewel of the gospel. The Holy Spirit inspires nature and fills man with this glorious resurrection hope. The more we have of the power of the Holy Spirit, the deeper and stronger are the convictions of the resurrection.

Reflection

What does Jesus' triumph over death mean to you? What difference does the resurrection make in your daily life and your future?

We Reap What We Sow

"I, the LORD, search the heart, I test the mind, even to give every man according to his ways, according to the fruit of his doings."

JEREMIAH 17:10

People can do many good things and yet not be holy in heart and righteous in conduct. They can do many good things and lack that spiritual quality of heart called holiness. Though good deeds may be done, they will be limited in scope and power if not performed in the name and spirit of the loving God.

How great the need of hearing the words of Paul guarding us against self-deception in the great work of personal salvation: "Do not be deceived, God is not mocked; for whatever a man sows, that he will also reap" (Gal. 6:7). What is sown in a godly, devoted heart will be reaped in a life of fruitful service.

Reflection

Pray and ask God to reveal any areas of your life in which you are sowing sin. Then ponder the sacrifices you are willing to make in order to live a holy life that reaps God's blessings.

Offer Prevailing Prayers

"Give ear to my prayer, O God, and do not hide Yourself from my supplication. Attend to me, and hear me."

PSALM 55:1–2

Like a brave soldier, who as the conflict grows sterner exhibits a more superior courage than he did during the earlier stages of the battle, so does the praying Christian, when delay and denial face him, increase his earnest asking and does not stop until prayer prevails.

Moses furnishes an illustrious example of importunity in prayer. Instead of allowing his nearness to God and his intimacy with Him to dispense with the necessity for importunity, he regards them as better fitting him for its exercise. When the Israelites set up the golden calf, the wrath of God waxed fiercely against them. Jehovah, bent on executing justice, said to Moses when divulging what He purposed doing, "Let Me alone!" (Ex. 32:10). But Moses would *not* let Jehovah alone. He threw himself down before the Lord in an agony of intercession on behalf of the sinning Israelites, and for forty days and nights fasted and prayed (Deut. 9:25). What a season of importunate prayer that was!

Reflection

To what degree have you kept asking God to meet particular needs? Why is it often hard to keep asking God to meet the same needs?

Subject Index

Scripture Index